EVOLVING CONSCIOUSNESS

IT'S MORE THAN A BOOK, IT'S A MISSION

CHRISTINA SAMYCIA, PSYD

From the Heart of Mt. Shasta Publishing

Christina Samycia, PsyD
483 Walnut St. Weed, CA 96094
www.christinasamyciapsyd.com

Evolving Consciousness/From the Heart of Mt. Shasta Publishing, 1st ed.
ISBN 979-8-9988322-0-8

To all the
lightworkers whose mission is
to create a new earth.

Table of Contents

Introduction

You must know in your soul that something huge is transpiring on the planet. Many believe that we are experiencing a massive evolution in consciousness. Although the world appears more dysfunctional than ever and that it is falling apart, we are really experiencing a global transformation. Because a crisis always precipitates evolution, the old world must fall apart to create a better one. We are currently experiencing the crumbling phase. If you are wondering what in the world is happening on the planet, this book will provide you with some answers. After reading this book, you will learn how to navigate this challenging, yet amazing time, receive valuable information to assist you in aligning with this evolution in consciousness and understand where we are heading as a collective.

Whether you believe in spirituality or not, it is undeniable that something transformational is occurring on the planet. In fact, many ancient civilizations predicted that this evolution would transpire at this time, which has been referred to as many different things including Age of Aquarius, 5-D Ascension, Kali Yuga and the Golden Age. The foreshadowing of this evolution was felt in the 1960's, which propelled many to begin their journey of self-exploration and spiritual enlightenment. This inevitably led to the questioning of our world including the systems we live in, collective beliefs and our social structures.

On the winter solstice in 2012, this momentum accelerated. If you recall, many ancient civilizations, such as the Mayans, prophesized that the calendar would end at this time, which marked the ending of the Age of Pisces, and the dawning of the Age of Aquarius. During the Age of Pisces, which lasted for approximately 2,500 years, we created hierarchical systems to provide structure and guidance for our lives. This resulted in the creation of most religions, political ideologies, and the world as we know it. This period was dominated by hierarchy and power because we mistakenly believed that we needed something or someone to believe in. As we shift into the Age of Aquarius, the universe is driving us to evolve our consciousness by embracing our sovereignty, empowerment, freedom, personal responsibility, and doing what is best for humanity.

Ever since 2012, many more have joined this movement of personal and spiritual exploration, as witnessed by the increase in interest in psychotherapy, self-help books, spirituality, metaphysics and astrology. Some important components of this exploration include examining our subconscious dynamics and all that we swept under the subconscious rug, understanding and changing our inaccurate belief systems, healing our wounds from our life experiences, recognizing and eliminating our cognitive distortions regarding our family dynamics, interpersonal relationships and social structures and ultimately changing how we think and navigate the world. Through this evolution in consciousness, we realize that we are no longer the victims of our circumstances, but the creators of our reality, which leads us to become empowered, self-reliant and sovereign.

As we continue further on this path of enlightenment, our scrutiny extends to the systems we are participating in including government, work environments and commerce. As a collective, we are moving up the pyramid of Maslow's hierarchy and making decisions based on self-actualization, not merely survival instincts, which leads us to make wiser choices. Because of this evolution, we are also moving beyond just accepting what is and are aspiring to something greater. And as the collective evolves, so must the systems we live in. This is why our systems appear to be crumbling because they are held together by dysfunctional ideologies and dynamics that many are no longer willing to tolerate, and our collective eyes are opening from our cognitive distortions.

In 2020, we had a huge contraction in this birthing process, which is just the beginning of many more to come. It is interesting to note that 20/20 symbolizes perfect vision. And ever since, more are waking up to the state of the world. We are seeing, with more clarity, the collective shadow as well as the illusions we have been programmed to believe. Because the condition of our planet can be seen as a projection of the collective consciousness, it is illuminating the consequences of our ego-driven life. The world appears dysfunctional as a way of illuminating our inner dysfunction, which has prompted many to question every aspect of our lives and the world we live in. We are seeing that the systems we live in are becoming increasingly more corrupt and are no longer serving us.

Because the darkness is being revealed, it is easy to get discouraged right now. However, the reason we are seeing so much darkness on the planet is that it needs to be revealed, not only to wake those up who have been asleep, but to make sure we do not repeat the same mistakes we have made for centuries. The dark needs to be brought to light to be transmuted. Although it is human nature not to want to see the unsavory truths, it is so important for our healing and evolution. Because just like in therapy, if we are to evolve, we need to bring all that we buried from our conscious awareness to the surface. Whether we are aware of it or not, we have all been traumatized by the narcissistic system that we live in. It is time for us to heal our collective wounds and create new paradigms of living, which will benefit all of humanity, not just a few.

As we evolve into a higher consciousness, we are moving out of ego into wisdom and love. This vibrational momentum is impacting all of us on some level. We all have a choice, right now, to move out of the confines of the current 3 D matrix, which is bound by ego, fear, greed, hate and suffering into a higher dimensional state. We are being asked to examine our stories, our ego selves, and evolve. And to live in this higher vibrational state, it is imperative that we work through our emotional baggage and upgrade our paradigms. This can be done by changing our limiting beliefs, working through our pain and traumas and becoming more mindful as to how we are living our lives. Because we are not victims in the world, but the creators of our reality, it is time for each of us to take responsibility over what we are contributing to the collective and make some radical changes.

During this evolutionary time, I believe that it is valuable to have a resource to traverse this challenging, yet amazing time. To create this new earth, we each need to do our work. We are all being called to work through lifetimes of trauma, clear old programming, upgrade our belief systems, align with this higher frequency and create new systems. Not everyone will be choosing to shift into a higher consciousness, but I believe in time, most will. It is no accident that each of us is here during this epic time. We are here to not only witness this evolution but create a blueprint for a new earth. We have the opportunity right now to manifest an idealistic world. Because light will always prevail, it is just a matter of time before we enter a new paradigm, but it won't happen on its own. There is no one coming to save us. The old system is crumbling, and we are here to rebuild it. It is up to us to stand in our power and create it. Together we can spark an evolution. This is truly a profound time in history!

When the moon is in the seventh house
And Jupiter aligns with Mars
Then peace will guide the planets
And love will steer the stars
This is the dawning of the Age of Aquarius

-Aquarius by the 5th Dimension

Preface

Mark Twain was noted for saying "The two most important days in your life are the day you were born and the day you find out why." I believe that the second day for me occurred on March 20th, 2020. For weeks, I was trying to wrap my brain around what was really happening in the world because I kept feeling as though there was a deeper spiritual meaning as to what we were experiencing. Despite my mental exhaustion, I headed to the lakefront path for my daily walk. About a mile away from home, I had an epiphany. This year was going to be pivotal within this evolution of consciousness! I felt a surge of energy run through my body and I was overcome with a sense of strength and purpose. It was then that I realized why I was here on this planet!

When I was a little girl, I knew that I would be part of a revolution of sorts. Not one of bombs and guns, but a revolution or more precisely an evolution of thought and now that day has finally arrived. This was the year that the universe was going to illuminate the matrix which was going to move us closer to transforming our planet. I have long believed that our 3-D matrix was held together by fear and ego and have become aware that our systems were becoming more ego-driven and corrupt. We have been lied to and manipulated for ages and this was the beginning of the end to all this. We were shifting into a higher state of consciousness, and the old system was going to fall apart. We are in the process of birthing a new earth, and this was just one of the many contractions. Although this situation appeared to be incredibly precarious, I trusted that everything was unfolding as it is supposed to because the universe never gives us anything we cannot handle. I knew, at that moment, that my purpose was to be part of this evolution in consciousness and that I was here to be one of the messengers.

Imagine there's no countries
It isn't hard to do
Nothing to kill or die for
And no religion too
Imagine all the people
Living life in peace
You may say I'm a dreamer
But I'm not the only one
I hope someday you'll join us
And the world will be as one

-Imagine by John Lenon

Chapter 1

Your Story

Introspection is paramount for our collective evolution. Although we would like to believe that we are logical, rational and conscious thinkers, science has shown us that anywhere from 80-99% of all brain activity is subconscious. Therefore, the subconscious mind holds more power and will override conscious thought. Because most of our brain activity is subconscious, it influences most of the decisions that we make. And because the foundation of our subconscious mind is created in our early childhood, it is important to understand this process.

When we were children, we created a story about ourselves and the world that is just not true. During our formative years, we created belief systems about ourselves and the world, based on our childlike perspective, limited life experiences and the beliefs of those around us. Based on our childhood experiences, we also endured emotional pain that we haven't fully processed, which is stored within our physical body. This story and the emotions attached to it becomes the building block of our cognitive and emotional foundation. We also have other information from our ancestors, parents and possibly past lives stored in our DNA that reinforces our story. To evolve, it is important for us to scrutinize this story and the beliefs that we hold and understand that there is an inaccurate script that is playing in our subconscious mind, which defines who we are, influences our lives and influences our decisions. This story shapes our perceptions, triggers emotional pain and we attract experiences that reinforce it. Unless we understand this story, process our emotional pain and rewrite it, we are unable to evolve into a higher state of consciousness.

To understand and change our story, it is important to accept that we are all wounded. No matter who we are, where we come from, what experiences we had, we have all endured emotional pain and carry the scars from our life journey. No matter what our gender, race, socio-economic status, we all suffer. Whether we consciously realize it or not, we all experience sadness, anxiety, anger, hopelessness, resentment and health issues. Our wounds are what we all share. On our journey here, we are all trying our best to cope with the suffering that comes with the human experience. All of us, to some extent, seek to escape our pain either through maladaptive coping mechanisms, such as the pursuit of pleasure, avoidance, minimization or distorting reality. But no matter how much we try to escape; our pain is still there. However, some of us have this inner voice; this inner knowing that speaks to us. This is our spiritual self, our higher dimensional self. This voice compels us to dig deeper and to look at our pain and dysfunctional dynamics because on some level, we know we can transcend them. Many of us have already started this. And in recent years, due to this vibrational influence, we are being triggered more than ever because we truly want to evolve.

It is paramount for our evolution in consciousness that we understand that we are spiritual beings having a human experience in this material world. Science has shown that we are energetic beings, not merely biochemical. And because you are a fractal of this interconnected energetic universe, you are connected to all and are more powerful than you can ever imagine. However, we have lost belief in this connection and our true power because of programming and life experiences.

Science has yet to unlock many aspects of our DNA, which has been labeled as junk DNA as well as much of our brain functioning, which may be the keys to our true powers.

This alignment with our spiritual energetic selves is the core foundation of this higher consciousness. You, the essence of who you are, is what we can define as consciousness, your spirit or soul. Science has measured that upon death, we lose 21 grams, which may be the measure of our souls. Because we are spiritual beings within a material body, we already have basic information and a set of belief systems that we bring into this world. We carry knowledge of our spiritual selves as well as a blueprint for optimal health. Some of these beliefs, which are in alignment with this higher consciousness, include that we are powerful, wise, whole, connected to all, safe, unconditionally loved and immortal. Our body knows how to function optimally and has information of how to grow and heal. We also bring in additional information that is encoded in our DNA from our ancestors, parents and past lives as well as information as to what we are to learn, accomplish and experience in this lifetime. Although we do not usually have conscious access to this information, as we continue through this evolutionary process, this information is coming to our conscious awareness.

Although we have an original program of perfection, once in the material body, this information becomes distorted. We begin gathering information through the experiences we encounter. We are receptive to our mother's, father's and others' feelings about us, their situations and views of the world. This is the beginning of the framework of how we view ourselves and the world. For example, if we had a narcissistic parent, we may learn that we are conditionally loved. If our parents had anxiety, we may learn that we are not safe in the world. These ideas conflict with our innate spiritual beliefs of being loved, safe and connected. To evolve into a higher consciousness, we must unlearn so many things.

We all have an ego, which represents the physical or 3-D material aspect of who we are. Part of this ego is the belief systems we created about ourselves based on how we interpreted a collection of events that happened to us. Our ego is a collection of thoughts, conscious and subconscious, about who we think we are, which is largely based on our childhood experiences and other programming that are highly inaccurate. However, who we are is not a collection of thoughts. Because we are not our thoughts, we are not necessarily who we think we are. This is quite a profound shift in how we probably think about ourselves because we tend to identify with who we think we are. However, if you were your thoughts, would you really be able to change your thoughts? Exactly, so, who is doing the changing? You are. You, then, are not your thoughts, if in fact you can change them. You have thoughts, as well as feelings, but they are not who you are. This may be a hard concept to grasp, because we tend to identify with the thinker.

You can look at this concept as though the ego is the participant, and you are the observer. Here is an example to illustrate this idea. You receive an email from a colleague who wants to meet with you. It may be that your first reaction is to get nervous and automatically jump to the worst-case scenario. You may begin to think that you did something wrong, which is part of your ego or your story. However, you, as the observer, can slow down this experience and observe the thoughts and feelings, and not attach to them. You can rationalize everything is ok and even if it isn't, you will be able to deal with it.

You are something much greater than who you think you are. Identifying with your thoughts leads you to be trapped in certain ideas about yourself, but at any moment, you can choose to just be who you are. And because you are not your story, you have the power to re-write it because this story keeps you trapped in suffering. You can evolve into higher states of consciousness when you allow the essence of who you are, your soul or spirit, not your ego, to be the navigating force in your lives. Although we need an ego to navigate our world, it is important not to allow the ego to define who we are.

During our childhood, because of our limited cognitive capacity, we create egocentric fantasies about why things happen. These speculations become the foundation of our belief systems. For example, if our parents were conflicted about our birth, we might form a belief that we are not wanted. Or if there was animosity within the household, we may blame ourselves and believe that the world is unsafe. Or if we were programmed to trust figures of "authority," we may not trust our inner wisdom. Many of these concepts are inaccurate. Although some of these beliefs may be conscious, most of this information gets stored in our subconscious mind. In addition, part of this subconscious mechanism is the biochemical and neurological response systems such as the fight or flight response attached to these experiences. These mechanisms all play a role in how our beliefs are shaped and how we respond to our environment.

As we continue to develop, we add to this framework of inaccurate belief systems and patterns of thinking and behaving, and it colors all the experiences we have on our journey. These belief systems and patterns influence every aspect of our lives. They influence how we think and feel about ourselves and the world and influences our behavior.

Additionally, we have unresolved emotional needs created by our formative experiences, which also becomes part of our subconscious emotional framework. We become energetically attached to these dynamics that were unresolved in childhood, and they replay in our lives. For example, if we felt conditionally loved, we may spend a lot of time and energy trying to get love and approval by overachieving or pleasing others. Or if we grew up in an unstable household, we may be overly preoccupied with needing to feel safe, which can possibly manifest in obsession and compulsive behaviors. Or if we were programmed to pursue a conventional life path, we might deny our true entrepreneurial desires.

As we go through life and encounter situations, whether we consciously realize it or not, we appraise these situations based on some of these inaccurate belief systems. We continue to use these inaccurate paradigms, which distorts our reality because we are applying past experiences to try to explain our present reality. This is problematic because our past experiences have nothing to do with our current reality. Therefore, we do not see reality as it is because we use our past experiences to interpret our current reality.

Some of our childhood experiences may trigger emotional pain such as fear, sadness, abandonment, shame, frustration and anger. This information conflicts with our original program of feeling happy, powerful, safe, connected and unconditionally loved. Researchers speculate that even as early as in the womb, we are receptive to the emotions of others within our environment. As an infant, when we were sad, angry or scared, we freely expressed and processed our emotions. As we grew older, we were taught to hold our emotions in. Theorists suggest that these suppressed emotions do not go away. These emotions become encoded within our physical body as cellular memory. When we encounter situations that resemble these experiences, whether we are conscious of it or not, this triggers emotional pain that is already there. For example, if you felt that your mother was emotionally unavailable and you did not feel as though you received her love and approval, whenever you perceive rejection or abandonment, it triggers this scar. This original scar may create a lifetime of chronic depression. If you had a significant trauma at birth, such as being born with the umbilical cord wrapped around your neck, this may create a lifetime of chronic anxiety and create a belief system that the world is scary, and I am not safe. As you evolve to a higher state of consciousness, the goal is clear these triggers to transcend the pain and suffering and embrace feelings of love, joy, safety and contentment.

As we travel on our life journey, we encounter situations that trigger emotional reactions. It is important to examine our triggers, which are also referred to as shadow work, which will be discussed in more detail later. These situations are neither "good" nor "bad" in themselves, but it is how we appraise these circumstances and the emotions it elicits that creates our distress. Although we usually blame our distress on external events, it is how we appraise these situations, consciously and subconsciously, and the emotions it elicits that cause our suffering. For example, if we do not get a job we want, it is how we appraise this that causes our suffering. We may become upset because we may misperceive that we did not get the job because we are not good enough or because nothing ever goes our way, which triggers emotional pain. Therefore, the situation of not getting the job did not lead you to feel upset, it is how you interpreted this situation. Whether we are feeling sad, anxious, angry or whatever else is disrupting our peace, it is how we are perceiving our current life circumstances that is triggering an emotional response which is only amplifying unprocessed pain that is stored in our body. Therefore, our suffering is internally created because it is how we appraise reality, consciously and subconsciously, and the emotions that it triggers that cause our distress. This is a very important concept to understand because one of the main paradigms shifts in this evolution in consciousness is understanding and working through our triggers and taking responsibility over our thoughts, feelings, actions and ultimately our lives.

Because suffering is created internally, the goal is to make changes to our perceptions, not to blame or fix external situations. External circumstances are neutral in nature. It is not until we judge them that they have meaning. These appraisals, rooted in a past reality, then triggers subconscious emotional pain; this pain is already there eliciting an emotional as well as a physical response. Again, we do not see situations as they are, but color it through the lenses of our past experiences. Because unprocessed pain amplifies this experience, it is important to process it.

Here is a Buddhist proverb to illustrate this. This proverb asks us to imagine that we are a glass of water and that there is a layer of sediment at the bottom that represents past painful emotional experiences that we haven't fully processed. External situations are the spoon that stirs up the water making it become cloudy. We believe the spoon clouded the water, but it didn't. If there was no sediment on the bottom, even when the spoon stirred the water, it would remain clear. Therefore, we need to clear out this sediment by working through, as much as we can, our painful experiences. We can also work on understanding that external situations may be triggering past emotional experiences in the moment and minimize our reactions, as well as process this trigger from the original trauma.

You have the power to change your belief systems on both a conscious and subconscious level and process the trauma that is stored in your cellular memory and feel empowered, at peace, content and joyful. You have the power to change how you appraise your reality and to determine better ways of responding rather than reacting to these situations. You also have the power to affect change in your world and the world around you. You are probably not aware that you created belief systems based on your childhood experiences, which are highly inaccurate and that you can change them at any time. It is so important to understand that many of the stress producing beliefs about yourself and the world are not necessarily true because these beliefs were created in childhood with your child-like lenses and limited life experiences. Although you created a story about yourself and the world, you have the power to rewrite your story and update your beliefs that are in alignment with this higher consciousness. Rewriting your story and changing your belief systems will be addressed on both a conscious and subconscious level. To align with this higher consciousness, it is important to understand and change these subconscious programs as well as heal and detach from subconscious trauma and process trauma that is stored in cellular memory. As we move into a higher consciousness, it is imperative that we work though our emotional baggage because we are not taking it into this new world we are creating.

Chapter 2

The Beliefs You Created

The belief systems based on our childhood experiences create our cognitive foundation and determine how we view ourselves and the world, which is not necessarily in alignment with this higher state of consciousness. This influences the decisions we make and the situations we create and attract within our lives. We carry this blueprint into our present and, until it is made conscious, addressed, and processed, it greatly impacts our lives. For example, if you grew up in an unsafe household, you may likely believe that the world is unsafe and may oftentimes project this concept onto the world around you. You may mistrust others or feel a sense of anxiety. If you felt unloved and rejected as a child, you may likely misinterpret how others treat you and/or primarily focus on examples of when others mistreat and reject you. You may also internalize a belief that you are not loveable or good enough, which will likely create feelings of hopelessness and sadness. If you grew up with parents who had many fears, it is highly likely you adopted those fears and they become part of the way you see the world, which can create chronic feelings of anxiety. These beliefs and emotions are not in alignment with this higher consciousness.

There are physiological reasons as to why your story is so powerful and difficult to change unless you make a conscious effort to do so. However, you do not have to be the victim of your story. You have the power to rewrite your story whenever you want. You just must believe that it is possible, fully understand it and start the process of rewriting it. Your thoughts are things. They are energy. Everything is energy. You, this book, the thoughts and feelings you are experiencing as you read this. All of this is energy. Our thoughts are energy created by the brain. The brain is built of tiny nerve cells called neurons. Neurons connect to other neurons and form a neural network. When neurons connect, they create a thought, which eventually imprints in our memory. The more we think the same thought, the more we reinforce this neural connection. This is a very important concept, because this explains why it is so difficult to change how we think and, consequently, how we feel, because our thoughts are "hard-wired" in the brain. This also explains our attachment to our ego self. We created a story that consciously and subconsciously replays itself and becomes hard wired in our brain. Think of your thoughts as habits; to break a habit takes time and intention. If you practice stopping or changing your thought, the neural connections become weaker. To evolve to a higher consciousness, it is important to become more mindful of your conscious and subconscious thoughts and feelings and to practice consciously changing them.

In addition to your thoughts being energetically hardwired, your brain is designed to register and perceive information that fits existing paradigms created in childhood. This makes it difficult to change our beliefs about ourselves and the world as adults. When we interact with the environment, our brain assesses the information at hand, and it will only see or interpret experiences based on our past experiences. Once we created a cognitive foundation in childhood, as an adult, it is difficult for our brain to store information that is unique because it automatically wants to categorize it into something with which it is familiar. In fact, information that does not fit what is already there is not registered. Our brain does this automatically and subconsciously before we have an opportunity to make a conscious correction. Our brain uses past information to interpret reality and can mutate it to fit these constructs. Using the previous example of feeling unloved or rejected as a child, you might misinterpret the action of others to fit this construct. You might dismiss when someone does accept you and shows you love. Therefore, you are not necessarily seeing what is really there. This explains how challenging it can be to change existing belief systems, but it can be done by expanding your paradigms and creating new ways of interpreting information and being more mindful of this process.

In addition to how our brain processes information, it is important to understand the power of the subconscious mind. We would like to believe that we are logical, rational and conscious thinkers. However, science has shown us that anywhere from 80-99% of all brain activity is subconscious. We can compare it to an iceberg. The tip of the iceberg is the conscious mind. The rest of the iceberg is the subconscious mind. Our subconscious mind has stored every experience we have ever had and the emotions they have elicited and registers everything. Most of our brain activity is subconscious and motivates the decisions that we make. Although we are consciously aware of a portion of our story, all of our story, even things we are not consciously aware of, is registered in the subconscious mind. This impacts how we react to and feel about our current experiences, as well as what we think and feel about ourselves and others.

The subconscious mind holds more power and will override conscious thought. For example, most of us can agree that being healthy is important but tend to engage in many unhealthy behaviors. You may have likely said "I know I need to eat healthy and exercise," which is a conscious thought, yet continue to engage in unhealthy behaviors. Because subconscious thought overrides conscious thought, these unhealthy behaviors are likely motivated by subconscious belief systems. For example, you may have a subconscious belief that you don't deserve to be healthy or that you actually want to be unhealthy because maybe that is how you received positive attention as a child. You might also likely have a belief system that you aren't loveable. In the case of weight issues, it is also possible that you felt unsafe in childhood and that you needed protection, which your body interprets as access weight. All these beliefs combined may override the conscious idea of desiring to be healthy. If you have tried changing your diet and incorporating an exercise program, but have been unsuccessful at maintaining long term change, it may be more effective to identify and change the subconscious programs, first, which will have more of an influence over your behavior. For example, when you realize that you deserve to be healthy or when you discover that you do not want attention for being unhealthy, you may begin to engage in healthier activities. Additionally, when you start to feel safe, your weight may change. Therefore, it is important to understand the belief systems that are stored on a subconscious level and make corrections to it.

Our brain also has an inherent mechanism to distort reality as to psychologically protect us from harm so that we can survive in our environment. Because some of the experiences we encountered in childhood created emotional distress and threatened our self-esteem, psychodynamic theorists claim that our subconscious mind creates defense mechanisms as a means of coping. Because we all felt vulnerable, innately inferior and encounter obstacles during our childhood, we created defense mechanisms to avoid our internalized feelings of vulnerability and inadequacy, which are our primary subconscious driver in our lives. As children, it was difficult to psychologically accept certain realities such as we weren't good enough, safe or unconditionally loved. Whether these speculations were accurate or not, the ramification of these realizations created intense anxiety and threatened our sense of self. Our brain then adopted ways of psychologically protecting ourselves. For example, if you grew up in a household where you were repeatedly told that you weren't good enough, this would lead you to feel sad and angry. Experiencing constant sadness and anger would not be a productive way to live. Therefore, your brain would create defense mechanisms to ensure psychological survival. These defense mechanisms become part of our subconscious framework.

According to psychodynamic theory, some of the most common defense mechanisms include repression, denial, projection, displacement, sublimation, rationalization, overcompensation, and reaction formation. Repression is a very common defense mechanism whereby our subconscious mind prevents disturbing or threatening thoughts from entering the conscious mind. Using the previous example of not feeling good enough, it is advantageous to repress these memories throughout your life. Having conscious access to these memories would not be helpful. All of us, to some extent, have repressed memories from our childhoods. Denial is similar to repression. This is when we block external events from awareness and refuse to experience it. When your parents are being critical, for example, you may just simply deny it is happening. Projection is when we attribute our own thoughts, feelings, and motives to another person. You may get unusually angry if someone is in adequate, when in fact, you feel inadequate and are not willing to see it. Displacement is the redirection of an impulse, usually aggression, onto a powerless substitute target. Because of your upbringing, this likely created anger, which may then cause you to be aggressive with others. Sublimation is similar to displacement but is a more constructive way to deal with our emotions. Creating art and journaling is a form of sublimation. Rationalization is when we cognitively distort the facts of an event to make the impulse less threatening. Overcompensation is when someone tries to make up for a perceived weakness by overachieving. Reaction formation is when a person goes beyond denial and behaves in the opposite way to which he or she thinks or feels. Someone who feels inadequate will gloat about achievements to make them appear better than they are. Our defense mechanisms are also responsible for our cognitive dissonance. Although these defense mechanisms protected us from emotional pain as children and into our adult life, many of these defense mechanisms are maladaptive ways of coping with our thoughts and feelings as adults and prevent us from accessing our true subconscious belief systems and processing our emotional pain.

In addition to defense mechanisms, transactional psychologists also have explained that due to our deep existential insecurities, we create patterns of relating to others which are also learned in childhood and embedded in the subconscious mind. As mentioned earlier, we are in essence a field of energy. According to Eastern philosophy, our innate energy levels are not usually optimal. We then seek out ways in which to raise our energy levels to optimal levels. When we interact with others, we essentially merge energy fields. A dynamic inherently occurs whereby there is an opportunity for an energetic exchange. Based on learned patterns, we sometimes take from or give energy to others. We have all experienced situations when we feel either drained or uplifted based on an interaction we experienced from another person.

Because most of our parents were imperfect and innately energetically deficient, they learned to maneuver the world seeking additional energy from other people including us. Based on our parents' story, unknowingly, they engage with us through what is called control dramas, which range from passive to aggressive forms of obtaining energy. For example, a passive example of a control drama is the victim strategy, whereby the individual seeks to gain attention and energy through the manipulation of sympathy. If a parent uses this strategy, this can cause feelings of guilt within a child and the child then gives energy as form of sympathy. The most aggressive form of control drama is intimidation, whereby the tactic of obtaining energy is through anger and hostility. If a parent uses this strategy, the child feels unsafe and drained. Depending on the control drama used by the parent and the innate temperament of the child, the child then adopts their own tactic of defending against and gaining energy. They may take a passive victim approach or a more aggressive bullying approach. Again, these patterns are learned in childhood and embedded in the subconscious mind. They play out in our relationships, as well as the systems we live in. It is very important for us to understand and uncover these control dramas because these dynamics keep us in lower vibrational states. As we align with a higher consciousness, we are moving out of these patterns of relating. Many of the systems we find ourselves in are rooted in these dysfunctional control dramas and as we change, so will these systems.

Individuals with narcissistic tendencies utilize control dramas as well as other dysfunctional ways of relating with others. In the last few years, there has been a significant increase of discussion regarding the concept of narcissism which may indicate that collectively we are examining the dysfunctional relationships within our lives and healing from narcissistic abuse perpetrated by our families, other people in our lives and society at large. When I use the term narcissism, I am not necessarily referring to Narcissistic Personality Disorder (NPD). Narcissism can be seen as a continuum. We all fall somewhere on that spectrum. Individuals with NPD fall on the high end of the spectrum. Narcissistic tendencies are created in early childhood to defend against feelings of inadequacy. Those high on the scale have a fragile sense of self, which leads to an overestimation of self-importance, a lack of empathy for others and a tendency to view others as objects. Within the family dynamic, highly narcissistic parents are unable to emotionally and sometimes physically care for a child because they tend to put their needs first. It appears that many are confronting the narcissists in their lives, stepping out of these dysfunctional relationships and healing from their wounds.

In addition to creating defense mechanisms and control dramas, according to an Adlerian perspective, we also create a life script, which is sometimes conscious, but often subconscious, as way of coping. Birth order is one factor that influences our life script. For example, an oldest child may have a natural inclination to take care of others and feel the need to achieve. Whereas the youngest may have a pattern of attention seeking behaviors and may be more irresponsible. These are not necessarily absolutes because every childhood dynamic is different. Sometimes, a younger sibling may take the more responsible role if the older sibling is struggling as a way of helping the family. These scripts are not inherently maladaptive because it is our innate feelings of inferiority that compel us to achieve great things in life. For example, a child who had a chronically sick parent, may decide to become a doctor as to resolve the anxiety of having a sick parent. However, if the unconscious motivators are not uncovered, they prevent us from accessing and correcting inaccurate beliefs and processing stored emotional pain.

The belief systems that are energetically held in the subconscious mind are continually reinforced, which will likely lead you to misinterpret them as truths. I refer to these as small "t" truths. Many of the beliefs that we think are true are merely opinions, which can be changed. There are very few truths that I refer to as big "T" truths. Truths with a big "T" are universal truths such as the sun rises in the east and sets in the west and matter cannot be destroyed nor created only transformed. Big "T" truths are absolutes, whereby everyone can agree on them. Small "t" truths are "opinions" that most of us adopt as true, usually at a very early age, because we don't challenge our belief system when we grow up. For example, the idea that "I am not powerful," "I am not good enough," "Doctors know best," etc. are a small "t" truth or opinions that we created in childhood based on our limited experiences. The concept of the "starving artist" is another small "t" truth. Some artists do financially struggle. However, some do not. Therefore, it is not a truth but an opinion. Many of these opinions are rooted in a lower vibrational consciousness.

As you start examining the beliefs that you hold, you may start to question these beliefs. Is that really true? A question I always challenge my client's with is "Says who?" If you are holding the belief that I am not good enough, ask yourself "Says who?" You may answer, "I don't feel good enough because I never felt like I received love and approval from my father. I was always disappointing him." Ok, but does that mean you are not good enough then or now? Why is your self-worth still measured by what your father thought then or thinks now? It doesn't have to. Just because your father said or implied some judgement of you does not make it true. You could right now decide that you are good enough, despite whatever your father may or may not have said. Again, this is an opinion of your father, not a truth. It is value to explore and change those small "t" truths that you hold on to a subconscious level because these concepts are causing you pain and are limiting you.

Another reason it is so important to understand and change these subconscious constructs is because our subconscious mind is not only misinterpreting reality and not seeing everything that is truly there but is attracting situations that support these subconscious beliefs. As mentioned before, our thoughts are energy and most of our brain power is subconscious energy. According to the law of attraction, we energetically attract circumstances that support the belief systems we hold on a conscious and more importantly subconscious level. Additionally, we subconsciously seek out situations that support our subconscious belief systems. This is based on an energetic principle that, energetically, like attracts like, which adds yet another level to how powerful the subconscious mind is. For example, you have likely noticed patterns in your life such as the people and situations you attract. You may have said, "I always seem to ________," fill in the blank; attract individuals that will abandon me, struggle with finance, etc. Again, these patterns likely stem from situations and beliefs that occurred in childhood. For example. If you felt like your emotional needs were not met by your mother, you will likely attract others that do not meet your emotional needs. Or if your family struggled with finances, you may likely find yourself in a similar situation. Therefore, to make real changes in your life, you will need to understand and change the beliefs that you hold in your subconscious mind, not just the conscious mind, detach energetically from them and create and reinforce new constructs.

Chapter 3

Your Emotional Experiences

As we evolve to a higher consciousness, we are moving out of lower vibrational states of fear, hate, victimization, despair, division and suffering into a higher vibrational state of peace, love, joy, empowerment, inspiration and cooperation. Now that you understand why you think the way you do, it is valuable to explore the emotions that are attached to your story that you are now processing and upgrading. As infants, we expressed emotions without restraints. As we grew up, we experienced situations that created feelings we likely suppressed. We store these unexpressed and unprocessed emotions in our physical energy field within our body. They affect our daily life and will manifest themselves sooner or later because how we consciously and subconsciously appraise current reality triggers these unprocessed emotions. It is also highly likely that these unprocessed emotions will surface even if not necessarily triggered possibly manifesting as sadness, anxiety or physical ailments. Therefore, it is important for you to explore and process the emotional experiences that are stored within your cellular memory.

We all have endured trauma on some level. Although most of us did not necessarily encounter devastating traumas such as wars, attacks, sexual assaults, etc., which I refer to as big "T" traumas. We all have encountered little "t" traumas such as being criticized by a parent, not receiving love and approval from a sibling and other hurtful and scary experiences from our childhood. These traumas are just as impactful as big "T" traumas and affect our day-to-day life. Yet, as adults we tend to minimize the emotions we endured in our childhood. One of the reasons we have emotions is to imprint events into our memory. This mechanism is paramount to our survival. As a child, if you attempted to place your hand on the stove and your mother yelled at you, for example, you would have been flooded with emotions. This would assist in solidifying this memory. Although in time this memory would likely be hidden from your conscious mind, unless you severely burned yourself, the subconscious memory would assist you in remembering that you should be careful around stoves. Although this mechanism is helpful in some cases, it is not advantageous if, for example, your mother was yelling at you about a lot of different things which were not necessarily important.

Our brain's information processing system has a natural tendency to process trauma so that it is no longer painful, but this system can be blocked by unprocessed trauma. It is speculated that it is during REM sleep that we process memories. You can compare your brain to a computer. As mentioned in the previous chapter, when information comes in, our brain needs to file it somewhere. It files it based on constructs already created. However, significant trauma, such as an attack, because this may be unfamiliar, the brain does not know where to store it. Because it is heavily encoded with emotional content, the brain also has difficulty discarding it. It then is not properly stored, which creates, so to speak, a glitch in the system, which is why individuals with severe trauma experience flashbacks, nightmares and other posttraumatic stress symptoms.

There is another type of prolonged trauma that creates a similar glitch in our brain's processing system. For example, if your father yelled at you occasionally, during REM sleep, you probably were able to process this small "t" trauma. However, if he yelled at you quite often and there was a lot of conflict happening at home, there might be too much content for your brain to process during REM sleep. These unprocessed memories would cause a similar glitch in the brain's processing system. These repeated situations can also create a conditioned response. You are probably familiar with Pavlov and his experiments with dogs. We similarly become conditioned. Taste aversion is an example of an affective conditioning method. If you became violently ill after eating tuna fish, for example, you will likely never be able to eat tuna fish again or at least for quite a while. If during your childhood, your father yelled at you quite often, it is highly likely you would have a conscious or subconscious emotional response to future authority figures. The good news is whatever the trauma, there are techniques to help the brain process this information, which is located in the Appendix.

You are probably not fully aware that you have trauma and emotional pain that is physically stored within your body. As you embark on self-exploration, it is important for you to truly connect to the feelings you experienced as a child and not minimize them. It is important to understand just how emotionally impactful your experiences were as a child. Research has shown that infants, even when given sustenance such as food and water, will not survive if not given love and nurturing. This is why painful childhood experiences are so deeply encoded within our body. No matter how trivial they may seem to us as adults, these emotional conflicts were incredibly painful for us as children, because they were so important to our survival. For example, if we were criticized or ignored by a parent, we may react with intense emotions such as sadness and fear because to an infant, not receiving love meant possible death. Additionally, some of our trauma may have occurred as early as prenatally, which is why it is important to have as much information as possible about your early childhood circumstances.

Our body not only has a biochemical makeup but an energetic one which needs to be in balance if it is to function correctly. Our energetic system is the precursor to biochemical reactions. This concept is not emphasized in our western culture but is the foundation of eastern medicine. Whether we are conscious of it or not, when present situations trigger unprocessed and unresolved emotions, it creates emotional pain that disrupts the energetic system, which then triggers a biochemical reaction.

Our body is wise. Our cells, organs, nerves and muscles know how to innately communicate. However, on our journey in the material world, we encounter several influences that disrupt this flow of information. We experience emotional and physical stress. We also encounter toxins, nutritional deficiencies, electromagnetic frequencies (EMFs), pathogens etc. that disrupt communication within our physical bodies. All these factors disrupt the flow of information within our body and are the antecedents to both physical and emotional illnesses. Our unresolved feelings and continually triggered emotional scars are not only contributors to emotional illnesses such as depression and anxiety but also impact our physical wellbeing because they disrupt our energetic and biochemical systems. Therefore, it is important to get in touch and fully process these emotions that are trapped within our energetic bodies.

When we interact with our environment, our brain subconsciously assesses the information at hand. We then have an emotional response to the situation at that moment.

These chemicals are created in the hypothalamus located in the brain. The brain creates a chemical that matches every emotion that we experience. When we feel an emotion, the brain assembles the appropriate chemical and then releases it into the bloodstream. There is a chemical for every emotion, such as anger, fear and sadness. Every cell in your body has thousands of receptor sites for all our emotions, and these chemicals attach to these receptor sites, which activate the cell and alter it. Each cell is alive and possesses consciousness, and it craves these chemical reactions. When we experience an emotion on a regular basis, our cell creates more receptor sites for that chemical, similar to how our cells change when we use of psychotropic drugs. If we become sad or angry every day, our cells will eventually crave sadness or anger. We then actually become addicted to those emotional experiences, similar to as to how we get addicted to our thought processes.

Because our cells are impacted by emotional experiences, intense emotional experiences can damage cells if they create an abundance of receptor sites that do not allow other important things to enter the cell, such as nutrients. This compromises our health and ages us, which is why dealing with your emotions is not only vital for emotional wellbeing, but physical health as well. You cannot separate the mind from the body because they work synergistically. Indeed, more and more researchers are speculating that a lot, if not most, of our illnesses are rooted in our emotional experiences, especially childhood trauma. This is why healing emotional scars is so important. We cannot sustain good health if we are continually experiencing lower vibrational emotions daily.

Stressors such as emotional trauma activates a series of complex nervous and biochemical communications that prepare the body's nervous, hormonal and immune systems to respond to impending or potential threats known as the flight or fight response. Here is how this mechanism works. Information from our environment is first registered by our senses via the brain stem and relayed to a portion of our brain known as the limbic system, which contains left and right temporal lobes or amygdala. If the amygdala determines that this new information is a threat, by comparing this to stored memories, it sounds an alarm and sends a report to the orbitofrontal cortex and then to the hypothalamus, which is the link to the nervous systems to the endocrine system via the pituitary. It first sends a message to the adrenals to stimulate the production of adrenaline which activates the sympathetic nervous system and creates physiological responses such as increased heart rate, muscle tension, etc. to prepare the body to fight or flee the situation. Then it signals the pituitary gland to produce Adrenocorticotropic hormone ACTH, which stimulates the adrenal cortex to produce cortisol. Cortisol activates the parasympathetic nervous system resulting in increased blood sugar and suppressed immune and digestive systems, which counterbalances the sympathetic fight or flight system to ensure that these systems do not become overstressed.

Although this system is advantageous when there is an actual physical threat, this mechanism turns on when there is a perceived emotional threat. When we experience chronic stress, this fight or flight response is continuously triggered and dysregulation will eventually occur within the endocrine system, primarily the hypothalamus, pituitary and adrenal systems. For example, if you grew up in an environment where your parents yelled often, when you would encounter yelling, this system is likely triggered. This becomes compounded and causes chronic dysregulation within the endocrine system and eventually the body starts to break down. Therefore, when we encounter a situation that resembles the original trauma, this will subconsciously trigger these sympathetic and parasympathetic responses.

In addition to the endocrine system, the lymphatic and immune systems play a role in the fight or flight response. Because we are not always able to fully process our emotions, it is speculated that unprocessed emotions start to collect in the lymph system just like physical toxins. When there is an excess of stress, the lymphatic system generates a reaction such as a fever to help release these emotional toxins from the body. Lymphatic reactions may help us process stressful emotional events so that we can let go and move on. The lymph system is made of several hundred lymph nodes. As lymph moves through the body, it absorbs and helps remove toxins, bacteria, digested fats, hormones and other waste products. It produces and stores white blood cells including t-cells that are responsible for destroying life-threatening pathogens. Your fighter B and T lymphocytes function in part by forming memories of specific pathogens. The immune system has a hard time distinguishing between those life-threatening pathogens and other new invaders that look similar. Using the example of chronic yelling in the house, the lymph system reacts to emotional threats that may resemble the original trauma, which leads to inflammation and suppressed immune system. This is just part of the physiological responses that occur from chronic emotional stress, illustrating just how important it is to process not only conscious emotional responses, but subconscious ones as well.

Theorists speculate that our DNA contains cellular memory from our ancestors, parents, and possibly our past lives that adds yet another dimension to our story because these memories reinforce our belief systems and compound our emotional experiences. As mentioned previously, our emotions are there to imprint experiences into memory as a way of learning. Traumas are coupled with intense emotional experiences and encoded in our brain and then passed down to generations to protect the lineage. For example, researchers have exposed rats to phobias that become apparent generations later. Researchers have also subjected rats to famine and the generations later the rats showed signs of obesity, because of an inborn fear of hunger. Based on this research, it is speculated that this also occurs in humans. Although this may have served a purpose in earlier years, this mechanism is no longer relevant or helpful. For example, famine is no longer a concern as it was for our ancestors. Therefore, it is no longer advantageous to hold the memories that may trigger our metabolism or behaviors to hold onto weight. If we had a lineage of financial scarcity, the fear of being poor, for example, is not helpful if we have access to resources. Keeping in mind the law of attraction, subconscious concepts of scarcity, whether it be resources, love, money or opportunities, will only make those things more difficult to attract in our lives.

In addition to ancestral lineage, our parent's experiences heavily impact us subconsciously and can create conflicts and repeated patterns. It would be logical to assume that their beliefs, patterns and traumas are even more impactful than ancestral information. If we are not mindful, we can even replay patterns in our lives. Sometimes, we get married or have children at the same time they did. We may develop illnesses or have a serious accident around the same age as a parent did. The good news is, you can stop these dysfunctional patterns by understanding them and processing them. Even more profound is by processing the traumas from your ancestors and parents, not only are you helping yourself, but you are also in essence helping the next generation and healing previous generations.

Many spiritual teachings subscribe to the concept of reincarnation. Because we are eternal spiritual beings, the material body we are inhabiting right now is only one of many. If we are eternal, it would only make sense that we experience many different lifetimes. Many of these experiences, especially painful and emotionally charged ones, also become encoded in our DNA. Whether it is true reincarnation that we are really inhabiting other bodies, or just memories of ancestral memories stored in our DNA, it may not really matter. The important concept to understand is that we come in this lifetime with preprogrammed data that is stored in our genetic material, such as emotional memories of death, love, loss and so many different human experiences. This emotional memory as well as belief systems that were learned in these lifetimes become part of our subconscious process that influences our lives. For example, some of our phobias are rooted in past lives. If you drowned in a past life, you might have a fear of water, which can be processed through techniques such as regression hypnosis. If there was something unresolved in a past life, such as you were not able to rescue your child from harm, you might have an unhealthy feeling of being overly responsible for that person in your present life which may have returned as a parent. If there is a karmic pattern of betrayal by loved ones, you may have anxiety and paranoia in your present life. However, all these patterns can be cleared.

The emotional pain from these traumas along with the belief systems that were created because of them, also impact our daily life even if these experiences never actually happened to us because they are physically registered in the body. This is why some of our belief systems and emotional pain do not always make sense. Some of us have phobias we don't understand, attachments to people and concepts and feelings of familiarity to certain situations, places and ideas that are just not logical. Therefore, it is important to understand that these memories and the belief systems created serve to amplify the emotional experiences we have from this lifetime. As you continue your evolutionary journey, you might find it helpful to understand the other stories that are part of your subconscious program. It is important to understand the full picture because some of these traumatic memories influence us in a deep way and add to our suffering. Sometimes, they are just as impactful as traumas that have occurred to us in the present day.

Another factor that impacts our emotional wellbeing and influences our belief systems are the underlying ideologies of the system that we live in. Growing up in a narcissistic household, whereby our emotional and/or physical needs were not met, and we were objectified by our parents, has been shown to result in depression and anxiety. Therefore, one would assume that living within a narcissistic system also plays a role in our emotional and physical wellbeing. It is becoming increasingly evident that most of the policies and prevalent societal beliefs of the United States are highly narcissistic, meaning that those who have fiduciary duties within our systems tend to be self-serving, objectify others and lack empathy and our policies are not benefiting the collective.

If you are born in the United States, you are likely born into a family who cannot afford for one parent to stay home and take care of you. Most mothers barely receive any paid maternity leave. In other developed nations, mothers receive one to two years of paid maternity leave because the collective ideology recognizes that the first two years of a child's life is critical. Therefore, in the United States, we start out in the world not feeling supported or valued by the system. As you are developing, unless your parents are aware, can afford to buy healthy organic food and have the time to prepare it, you are consuming food that has been tampered with, synthetic, potentially poisoned and lacks nutritional value. You are also breathing polluted air and drinking contaminated water. This illustrates that the system is not ensuring that what you are consuming is safe. In fact, in the United States the FDA allows 10,000 ingredients within our foods, but Europe only allows 400, deeming the rest as harmful to our health, which is just one of the differences in policies.

Then you grow up, go to school and then off to college, where you incur a significant amount of debt. You have not even moved out on your own and started working and you are already financially at a deficit. In other developed nations, college is free. College tuition has also exponentially increased in the last few years, again illustrating the exploitation of the consumer. You then get a job, where you are essentially exploited by the CEO who is making millions, but you are struggling to make ends meet. You are also required to work forty plus hours at a job that you do not love, at a fraction of the pay compared to those at the top, to make other people rich and fulfilling other people's dreams, not your own. The motto of most companies is highly likely profits over people and there is huge pressure to produce and succeed. You have very little time off and are made to feel guilty if you take it, whereas the average European, for example, receives six weeks minimum of government mandated paid vacation per year. You are stressed by the cost of living, which has also only been exponentially increasing.

The prevalent ideology, especially in the United States, is to work harder, achieve more, consume more, but to what end. It appears many are spending most of their time working to merely survive, not thrive. Additionally, a large portion of your paycheck is going to healthcare, which is also astronomical compared to other nations where healthcare is free. We are the only country where the number one reason for bankruptcy is medical expenses. And then you pay approximately thirty percent of your paycheck to the government, where you are gaslit in believing that in supposedly the riches country, we cannot solve poverty, but we have a huge military fund and are able to send money overseas. You are also aware that the government is working for corporate interest, not yours. These are just a few examples of policies that one would label as narcissistic and are negatively impacting all of us. The underlying feelings of living in this system creates anxiety, as well as feelings of isolation and not being supported, which may be why, compared to other developed nations, United States has a higher percentage of mental health issues as well as higher suicide rates.

In addition to unresolved emotional material that remains unprocessed in cellular memory, there are other factors that can trigger emotions such as sadness and anxiety. Just like the body creates pain to alert us that something is wrong physically, our emotions can also be an indication that there is problem in our life. Sometimes, our intuition is registering something in the environment and is creating an emotional response to alert us to a situation that might be potentially harmful or dangerous. If you are experiencing dread about going to work, for example, it may be that something in your work environment, such as the people, environment or other unhealthy dynamics are present. Your dread may also be an indication that this job or the work you are doing is no longer right for you. Or if you are in a relationship with a person that is harmful to you, you may begin to experience unexplained sadness. As we continue our evolutionary journey, our intuition with likely increase.

There is a small population of individuals referred to as empaths, who feel the emotions of others. Because of this, empaths may experience emotions that are not necessarily theirs. Not only do empaths feel the emotions of others, but they can even feel physical pain of others. Empaths are also usually highly sensitive. They can be overstimulated by bright lights, loud noises, crowds and environmental chemicals, which may trigger an emotional response. Some of the tools within the Appendix can be useful to help process these emotions.

When we are not following our spiritual or life path, the conflict between the ego and spiritual self can also create feelings of despair and anxiety. Because we come into this lifetime with information as to what we are to learn, accomplish and experience, our subconscious alerts us when we are deviating from this path. I believe that as we continue this evolutionary path, more of us will be experiencing this type of distress because a primary component of aligning with this higher consciousness is aligning with our spiritual self and fully embodying our spiritual mission on this planet.

Hormone and neurotransmitter disruption can also be exacerbating our emotions. Our emotions can also be impacted by a disruption in our gut health, pathogens including heavy metals, parasites, bacteria and viruses, as well as other physical imbalances. Nutritional deficiencies can also impact how we feel. These are some things to keep in mind as we start the process of self-discovery because it is wise to get clarity on the sources of your distress.

Chapter 4

Exploring and Understanding Your Story

One of the steps in evolving your consciousness is to begin exploring and fully understanding your story, which will help clarify the belief systems you have created, how you are appraising your current reality, and the emotional pain that is triggered. You are now aware that many of the beliefs about yourself and the world are not true and not aligned with this higher consciousness because these beliefs were created in childhood with your child-like lenses and limited life experiences. Therefore, many of your beliefs are opinions, not truths and can be challenged and changed. Before you can start upgrading your story to be aligned with this higher vibrational consciousness, it is important to start exploring your story and identifying belief systems that are no longer serving you on a conscious and subconscious level, as well as identifying the emotional pain they trigger.

Starting a journal is an excellent way to accomplish this. You can begin the journaling process by writing the narrative of your story to discover the conscious and subconscious beliefs that you are carrying, as well as any emotional trauma that may be stored in your cellular memory. It is important that you write out this narrative and all future journaling rather than type it because handwriting provides you with better access to subconscious material. Handwriting your journaling can also be cathartic, which is quite beneficial. When drafting your narrative, it is valuable to start this story prenatally, if possible. When you begin your narrative, start with the beginning of your story, the time between conception and birth. Located within the Appendix are some questions you may want to answer to help you fill in all the details of your story, which can lead you to a better understanding of the details of your story. In addition to your story, it is also helpful to gather information regarding your parents' stories and even grandparents' stories.

After you have gathered information regarding your story and the stories of your parents and ancestors, you can begin uncovering your conscious and subconscious belief systems as well as any emotional trauma that may be stored in your cellular memory. Here are some examples. If you had a birth trauma, this could explain chronic anxiety. Maybe your mother felt conflicted about having a child. This could create a belief system of not feeling wanted, which could lead to chronic feelings of sadness. Maybe your birth created anxiety within the family due to financial strain. This may create a belief system of feeling overly responsibility for situations and guilt. Maybe your siblings did not welcome a new child. This could create a belief of not being loveable and feelings of sadness and abandonment. When you start writing out a narrative, you will likely start to notice patterns. These patterns will lead you to beliefs that may be stored on a subconscious level. Take some time to examine this narrative and start to identify the beliefs about yourself and the world that were created because of this story and the emotions these experiences elicited so that you can now start challenging and changing them.

After you have journaled the narrative of your story and started identifying some belief systems that you would like to change and some unprocessed emotional trauma you would like to clear, you can also choose to keep a daily journal to continue assisting you further in uncovering subconscious beliefs and unprocessed emotional material. You may choose to start your journaling by exploring situations that are creating distress in your life now and identify how you might appraise them based on your story and the subconscious belief systems that are triggering emotional responses. It may be helpful to take some time to write down the circumstances in your life that are creating distress as well as identifying the emotions that they are triggering. Once you have written several situations down, examine the one that is creating the most distress. Become clear about your thoughts and feelings regarding this situation and start writing them down without judging or minimizing them. Now, based on your childhood experiences, determine where these thoughts and feelings came from. Ask yourself the following questions: "How am I viewing this situation?" "What feeling is this situation triggering? Why?" "Where did I feel this before," "Why am I perceiving the situation the way I do," and "Based on what I learned about my story, what are some belief systems that I hold that are resonating with this situation?"

Here are some examples that may be helpful. Let's say you notice in your journal that you become irrationally upset, anxious and sad when things are not going perfectly in your life. You may realize that your constant striving for perfection is causing you stress. When you ask yourself why is being perfect important, you realize that you created a belief system in childhood that you needed to be perfect to receive love because you never felt as though you could please your parents. Therefore, a belief you may choose to work on is "I am not lovable or good enough" and the emotion you may choose to process is sadness. In another example, you may also notice that you become unreasonably upset when your partner is not listening to you. You may ask yourself, "Why is this upsetting me so much?" You may remember that there was significant chaos in your family, and you often felt invisible, which triggers feelings of abandonment and anxiety and created a belief that "I don't matter" and "I'm not important". Or in another example, you may find that you are struggling with your boss, who is authoritarian and demanding. You notice that you react and become distraught any time she would offer constructive criticism. You are reminded that this resembles the dynamic with your own hard-to-please authoritative father. This situation elicits feelings of sorrow and inadequacy, as it dredges up your old emotions of your father.

It is important to link your past emotional experiences and the belief systems that contribute to this distress. Then repeat the process with the other situations you wrote down. Practice linking the past to the present to understand why you think and feel the way you do. Use the narrative you created as a reference for your further journaling. You can now start the process of change by understanding how and why you think and feel the way you do. Now that you are becoming more conscious of your thoughts and feelings, you can start the process of relating them back to their origins. By re-examining your past, you can see how it has shaped your present. Therefore, it is important to find that link to the past that explains why you feel and think the way that you do now; this is the key to better understand your full story.

As you continue journaling, it may be helpful to also explore any childhood memories that trigger negative emotions. These memories are the keys to unlocking themes that may create emotional pain as well as unprocessed emotions. In the next few sections, you will learn some techniques to help process some of the emotional pain from these memories. As mentioned earlier, during this process, ask yourself the following questions: How did these childlike experiences mold my emotional experiences? How did these experiences shape how I see myself and the world? What belief systems did I create because of some of these experiences? As you start to recall these memories, imagine yourself as a child reliving these experiences to really identify how you felt without minimizing or denying your feelings.

As you continue journaling for a while, you will also start to notice patterns. For example, are you attracting similar circumstances or people into your life? Are you noticing that you often struggle with the same issues such as finances, relationships, work, health, etc.? Do you notice recurring feelings of depression, anxiety or anger? These patterns are clues to subconscious belief systems that you likely hold. Again, some of these belief systems may not be logical or rational based on your current life experiences because they may have been created by a parent, ancestor or a past life.

Patterns in relationships are especially helpful to understand what is occurring subconsciously. Understanding the feelings that result from the dynamics in your relationships can also lead you to understand your scars from the past because we often choose relationships with others to resolve past psychological conflicts. We tend to pick significant others, friends, coworkers and acquaintances that resemble our parents, siblings or other significant individuals from our past, which can reflect our unresolved unconscious desires and needs. Although most of us understand that relationships with our parents play a role in future relationships, other significant relationships, such as siblings, are just as influential. We are attracted to others because the dynamic feels familiar. Moreover, we want to emotionally "fix" the things we were unable to fix in our past. Because we did not satisfy an emotional need that was established in our earlier years, we try to get it from the people in our present life, but this only leaves us frustrated, hurt, and disappointed when it invariably is not met. We also find it difficult to leave these dysfunctional relationships, because we have this psychological need that has not been met. This dynamic may prevent us from having healthy relationships.

For example, if you felt rejected by a parent, you will likely seek out individuals similar to that parent who will likely reject you. You may tend to continue to stay in these relationships hoping that you will finally get the love and validation that you have been seeking. Or if you had a younger sibling that was always needing help, you might likely seek out a relationship where you find yourself constantly helping that person. Although this may make you frustrated, you will likely continue this dynamic because it is familiar and that there is a subconscious wish to fix this person. It is also highly likely that you built your self-esteem around being the more responsible sibling that was always there to help, which may also keep you trapped in this dynamic. Here are some questions you may ask yourself. What patterns are you uncovering in your current relationships? How are they linked to your childhood relationships with your mother, father, siblings and other significant relationships from childhood? What belief systems are playing out through these dynamics? What emotional pain are they triggering?

One of the things to keep in mind is that when you begin examining your past, as well as how you think, feel, and behave, it is important that you observe, not judge it. Being judgmental about how you think, feel, and act or have acted is not productive. Your job is to be the observer, not to be critical of what happened, how you reacted or of how you think and feel about it. It is also important that you observe your past without minimizing it. When you examine your past, you may think "It wasn't that bad," or "It's understandable why things happened the way they did," or "My parents treated me the way they did because of the circumstances that they were having." You may also think, "It's in the past, and there is nothing I can do about it." However, to really understand what is occurring on a subconscious level and to truly process it, it is important to not minimize or rationalize the events that happened. It is important to get in touch with how you felt as a child during this experience.

As we continue our journey, feelings of sadness, anger, anxiety, etc. will arrive, but these emotions are perfectly normal and healthy. It is important to feel the feelings to process them. Although the goal is to feel peace, joy and contentment, it is so important to acknowledge the feelings that arise and not bypass, minimize or rationalize them. They will pass. When you are honest with how you think and feel, you may feel vulnerable, which is not to be confused with weakness. However, some people believe that feeling emotions makes them "weak," which can be an obstacle in self-exploration. One of the reasons that we think expressing emotions is a sign of weakness is that we don't fully understand them, which is why our emotions have sometimes been painful in the past.

Emotions are part of who we are, and it is important to feel comfortable feeling and expressing them. We might also have seen others displaying emotions inappropriately and perceive them as being unstable. However, it is important to remember that feeling your emotions is not necessarily being overwhelmed by your emotions, and even if you are, this is ok. By avoiding your emotions, by stuffing them inside because you are afraid of them, is not much different from an overly emotional display. It is just the opposite end of the same spectrum. These emotions will eventually surface sooner or later. Even if you attempt to avoid them, they are still being triggered and impacting you in a negative way. It takes a strong person to be able to go back and look at the past and oneself honestly. We all feel hurt, sad, scared, disappointed, and vulnerable and just because we have these feelings does not mean we are not strong and secure. Having feelings is a natural part of being human. Therefore, the healthiest and strongest place is to feel and express your emotions in a healthy way.

As we continue along this evolution in consciousness, the vibrational energy is pushing more and more of our suppressed emotions to the surface for them to be processed and cleared. Because of this, we have been experiencing tremendous growing pains for the last few years, which has also been impacting us physically and emotionally. We have also been experiencing solar flares and other vibrational frequencies on the planet. Some believe that these solar flares are infusing us with light, which are pushing our shadows and traumas to the surface for us to process them and transmute them into light. Light also carries information. These solar flares are also upgrading our physical bodies so that we can be in alignment with this new consciousness. It is also speculated that our DNA is even changing.

There are many ways in which you can process and clear the emotions that come up, as well as dysfunctional beliefs you would like to clear, which are included in the Appendix at the end of this book. Various techniques that you can do on your own are illustrated such as meditation with self-energy healing, Emotional Freedom Technique (EFT) and

The Script Meditation, as well as techniques that you can be facilitated by a therapist such as hypnotherapy, Neuro-emotional technique (NET), Eye Movement Desensitization and Reprogramming (EMDR) and Holographic Memory resolution (HMR).

Another obstacle to self-exploration is that you may fear that if you explored your emotions, you might find something wrong with you. Our lack of knowledge about our emotional lives prevents some of us from self-reflection. However, everyone experiences emotional pain. Everyone at some point in their lives feels sad, anxious, angry, frustrated, lonely, etc. This is part of the human experience. Because our emotional self is so personal to us, it is highly vulnerable to scrutiny. The idea that "I am not feeling okay" has, in some ways, been misconstrued to mean, "I am not okay." This is because it is difficult to separate our feelings from who we are, but it is important to realize you are not your feelings. Your feelings are just a part of who you are. There does not have to be a stigma attached to having and exploring these feelings. I find it interesting that, in our society, we do not have a problem going to a doctor if we have a physical ailment, but we feel that we need to struggle alone with our emotional needs. It may be that we do not view our physical health as personally, but having a physical ailment is not any different than feeling depressed or anxious. It could be that physical ailments are viewed differently from psychological ailments because we are not taught to believe that everyone suffers and that our emotions are biochemical reactions. Furthermore, many of our physical ailments are caused by emotional trauma. Therefore, it is important to put our emotional wellbeing in perspective and deal with it just as we would deal with any physical ailment.

Additionally, we fear that the discovery of a dysfunctional childhood would be reflected poorly upon us. Some of us feel ashamed of our childhood experiences. However, you are not the sum of your experiences. Everyone has a dysfunctional childhood to some degree. When we were children, we were, to some extent, victims of our situation because we were unable to make the choices that we can make as adults. We also did not yet have the tools we needed to cope with these situations. But at any moment, you can choose not to continue being the victim of your past and change how you think, feel, and act once you understand the process. Your past does not have to define who you are in the present. You are who you choose to be in the present and you can decide who you want to be in the future. We have all been scarred by the past. This is what we all share. Our past creates emotional scars, and personal growth is the process of uncovering and healing those scars. This is nothing to ever feel ashamed of, no matter what has happened to you.

Now that you have examined some obstacles to self-exploration, as you continue with your journaling, you will start to identify some belief systems that you created that are triggering emotional pain. Here are some common beliefs that most of us struggle with, which are rooted in the 3-D reality: I am a victim, I am not powerful, I am not good enough, I am not loveable, I don't deserve to be happy or to get what I want, I am all alone, I don't belong. I am not safe. I can't trust anyone, People are always hurting me, treating me poorly, etc., I can't create the life I want and Money, love, [whatever you desire] is hard to get or keep.

Remember, these beliefs are opinions, not truths and can be changed at any time. These beliefs are not aligned with a higher consciousness and are triggering emotional pain and hurting you. They keep you stuck in a lower vibrational frequency and prevent you from aligning with a higher consciousness. Now that you have explored your story and started identifying some belief systems that you hold as well as identifying the emotional pain that they trigger, it is time to look at some upgraded paradigms.

Chapter 5

Evolving into Empowerment

Now that you understand that the subconscious belief systems you hold about yourself and the world were created during your formative years, which influences most of your decisions and you now have a deeper understanding of your story by identifying your inaccurate belief systems, the emotions they elicit, and dysfunctional interpersonal dynamics, you are ready to begin making some paradigm shifts that are more in alignment with this higher consciousness. Integral components of this evolutionary process are emotionally growing up, resolving the subconscious wishes and desires of your internalized child, taking responsibility over your life, letting go of the illusion that the external world is there to take care of you or make you feel better, understanding that only you can resolve internal conflicts and accepting that you are responsible for your own happiness, contentment and the outcome of your life.

Evolving out of victim-consciousness into empowerment, embodying your sovereignty and understanding that you are powerful are the most important paradigm shifts in this evolution in consciousness. Although we are programmed to believe that the external world is more powerful than we are and that we are victims of our reality, a major paradigm shift is to start embracing just how powerful you truly are. I should preface that the concept of being powerful is not power over others, but an inner power; power over yourself and your life; your creative power. Additionally, being powerful is not necessarily having significant wealth either. Unfortunately, many spiritual teachings overly fixate on this concept of manifestation of material abundance, which is still part of this old paradigm. Seeking to have power over others and being obsessed with material wealth stems from a subconscious feeling of inadequacy and is not true power at all. Because you are a fractal of this interconnected energetic universe, you are connected to all, have unlimited creative potential and are more powerful than you can ever imagine. You are only limited by the programming you received and the beliefs you hold, which you have the power to change. You are the creator of your reality, not a victim within the world. You chose to come here to fulfill a unique destiny and have amazing gifts to offer. You are wise, resilient, and amazing!

Although it is our internalized child, in addition to the subconscious beliefs we carry and the programming we internalize, that believes and feels as though he or she is a victim, which was true at one time, this only continues to be true if you believe it to be. And being powerful can be as easy as just making the choice to be so. Bruce Lipton, biologist and author of the Biology of Belief said, "Our beliefs control our bodies, our minds and thus our lives." You are likely familiar with such sayings as "Mind Over Matter," or "Whether you think you can or you can't, you're right," as well as an abundance of research behind the placebo effect, which confirms that we are powerful, and that our beliefs hold tremendous power. Our thoughts create our world, and our collective thoughts create and influence our collective systems.

One way in which you are powerful is that although you may not always have control over all the circumstances in your life, you always have a choice in how you respond to them. Nothing has power over you because nothing can make you think or feel a certain way. As I mentioned earlier, if something triggers you, these are your triggers, which you can work on. And keep in mind, stress is internally created. When you are in a situation that triggers sadness, anger, anxiety, you can pause, then take a deep breath and then ask yourself the following questions: Why am I feeling this way? What is this situation triggering in me? How am I viewing this situation and why? How can I look at this in a different way? This is empowerment.

Here is an example to illustrate this. Let's say you notice that you become stressed when you attempt to do something, such as create a presentation for work, and it does not turn out as well as you would have wanted. When you examine this, you realize that you feel stressed, sad, and anxious when you believe that things aren't going perfectly. After looking at your thoughts, try to understand where they originated. Then stop, pause, and ask yourself: What emotional scar is this situation triggering? In this case, it might be that you inaccurately believe that to receive love and approval from others, you need to be perfect. Your unhappiness may have been created because you did not feel as though you received approval from your parents. Striving for perfection is exhausting. You can believe that you are ok even if you are not perfect and that you are no longer the little child that desires approval.

It is helpful to start taking ownership over your thoughts and feelings through self-examination and awareness. Understanding conscious and subconscious dynamics will empower you as you begin to understand why you think and feel the way you do. When you become more aware of your emotional life by understanding it and bringing it to consciousness, this will start to give you the ability to change your perceptions and reactions and ultimately feel more empowered. You have an opportunity right now to take charge of your life. When something happens and you feel sad, disappointed, hurt, or anxious, you can choose to believe that you are powerful and understand why you think and feel the way you do and feel something different.

Earlier I stated that we may not always have control over all the circumstances in our lives; however, I do believe that we contribute to some, if not most of the circumstances that we attract into our life. We are definitely co-creators of our reality, which is another example of how powerful you are. We create our reality by the beliefs we hold and the emotions we feel, both conscious and subconscious. However, we should not blame ourselves for the situations we are in but take responsibility over them. Therefore, if you are in a situation that is undesirable, instead of taking the victim position and asking, “Why is this happening to me?” it is more empowering to ask, “What subconscious programs do I have that attracts this dynamic to me?” or “What am I supposed to learn from this situation?”

As mentioned previously, we attract some circumstances in our lives based on our subconscious and conscious belief systems. We also attract situations because there is a life lesson we need to learn through this experience. There is a basic metaphysical principle referred to as the law of attraction. We live in a vibrational world. Our thoughts and feelings are energy. Like energy attracts like. The thoughts we focus on consciously and more importantly subconsciously attract similar experiences into our lives. Science has shown us very interesting evidence that suggests just how powerful we are. According to quantum physics, all matter exists in a wave of possibilities. It is only when the observer, the “I,” fixates on a point that it materializes. Therefore, without the observer, even material objects would not exist as we know it.

It is only when we perceive something that it actually begins to exist in reality. This has profound implications for how powerful we are. This perspective can help you shift from victim to creator of your life.

When we want to change the circumstances in our lives, most of us tend to look at what we can change externally. However, a more effective way of changing your circumstances is to change your conscious, and more importantly, subconscious beliefs. When you change your thinking, your external reality changes. For example, if you find yourself struggling with finances, before focusing on finding a better job, or starting a budget, it's more advantageous to first understand and shift your belief systems about money. If you believe that money is evil, or that money is difficult to obtain, this prevents you from attracting and/or holding onto money. Once you shift your beliefs, your behaviors will change and the situations you attract in your life will as well. Therefore, it is important to make a shift from being the victim to taking responsibility for the reality that you are creating. By making changes in how you think and the beliefs you hold on a conscious and subconscious level, you can create a different reality. You will start attracting and manifesting new situations.

Because the universe mirrors for us what we believe on a conscious and more importantly subconscious level, it is so important to become aware of these subconscious programs and start to change them as well as becoming more mindful of the things we say and think and even the messages we expose ourselves to because this can reinforce belief systems we want to shift. Start paying attention to the things you say out loud and to yourself and start the practice of reframing them. Keep in mind, the subconscious mind is very powerful. It hears everything. What are the things you say to yourself or out loud on a regular basis? What messages are you exposed to daily? Are they fear-based or negative? This impacts your reality. This can be difficult to avoid because there are so many fear-based messages that we are exposed to on a regular basis. However, when you start becoming more mindful, you will likely start noticing how frequently we are bombarded by fear-based messages. Hopefully, you will become more mindful of the information that you allow into your life.

For example, watching the news is very anxiety provoking and reinforces our fears. The media reinforces that idea that the world isn't safe by reporting crimes, terrorism and other atrocities. Additionally, our medical community is not promoting "wellness," but promoting illness. Instead of sending messages of good health, we are inundated with fear about contracting cancer, heart disease or diabetes. We see commercials regarding drug interventions and other treatments. By focusing on these constructs, this subconsciously promotes ill health.

One phrase that keeps us stuck in the victim paradigm is "I have to... (fill in the blank)." For example, many say, "I have to work at this job because I have bills to pay," or "I have to stay in this situation because there is nothing else I can do." Remember, everything is a choice. There is truly nothing you ever have to do. We always have hundreds of other options but don't always see them. Oftentimes, we use this phrase because it's a subconscious program that keeps us stuck in these situations. In addition to the phrase, "I have to...," I have noticed is the overuse of the word "stressed." It appears we label everything as stressful, work, life, relationships, the holidays. This is a victim-based concept. Life can be challenging, but things do not have to be stressful. They are only stressful when we label them so. Be mindful of overusing this word. If you find yourself in a challenging situation, before labeling it as stressful, breathe and reframe. You can tell yourself that you will get through this situation, and everything will be ok. Remember, you are powerful!

You have the power to find peace even amid adversity by practicing radical acceptance. A way in which we can shift from feeling like a victim to being empowered is by practicing radical acceptance. One reason that most of us are not feeling at peace is that we are judging and not fully accepting our current circumstances. We tend to label our current situation as either good or bad. Situations are neither good nor bad, it is how we label them that makes it so. Buddhist philosophy emphasizes that our suffering is created by our desires and expectations, but once we accept the present moment exactly as it is, our suffering ends, because we have no expectations of how it should be.

There is a prevalent idea in our western world that life should be a certain way. Most of us believe that life should be easy and that we should be happy all the time. However, life will sometimes be difficult, and once we can accept this idea, we can transcend our suffering. Being human means experiencing pain and encountering adversity. Part of staying in a higher vibration is accepting our current reality and minimizing the suffering, which is achieved by accepting it. There is a Buddhist saying, "Pain is inevitable, but suffering is optional." No matter how enlightened we are, we will all experience situations that create feelings of sadness, fear, anger, and frustration, but personal growth is about minimizing not the situation but the suffering. We suffer because instead of accepting our situation and understanding it, we appraise it, consciously and subconsciously, based on our story. Whether we consciously realize it or not, when something triggers an emotion such as sadness, for example after a breakup, we replay our story. Whether we are conscious of it or not, we begin to think, I'm not loveable, I can't do anything right, I'm all alone, which elicits and compounds the negative emotions. This is where we get into the loop of suffering. Inner peace can be found when we start practicing radical acceptance, which means understanding, not attaching to this story, letting go of suffering and accepting instead of judging our current circumstance.

Most of us have expectations of how things "should be, which can cause us distress. We have a picture of how our life should be, how our family should be, how others should treat us, how much money we should be making, what job we should have, etc. These expectations are what create our suffering because, frequently, our present does not resemble what we think it should. We become victims of the images we create and the thoughts that we have about how things should be, which creates un-peacefulness. We often judge how our present should be, but we miss out on appreciating the moment. If you accept your situation the way it is without judgment, you could eliminate your suffering. This does not mean that you should not try to change your situation, but it means that you can find peace within your present circumstances and make changes without emotional attachment, because judging your reality is truly not productive. When you realize you are not a victim in your life, you can learn to accept your current reality.

Many people worry or get upset about their situation, which is not facilitating anything positive. There is a difference between being concerned about our situation and worrying or being upset about it. Before we can make changes to a situation, it is important to accept it first. Because energetically, if we are not accepting it, we are adding to the negativity associated with the situation. This makes it difficult to attract something different. We don't have to necessarily like it, just accept it. Remember, you created these desires and expectations, so you can eliminate them. You are in control. Inner peace is achieved when we lose our attachment to our desires and can see the reality in our current situation without judgment. You can find peace and appreciate what is instead of lamenting what is not. Letting go of expectations and desires can be quite profound, leading you to feel at peace with your present and help you feel empowered.

Understanding that you can satisfy your own emotional needs is another way in which you are powerful. It is our victim paradigm that we mistakenly believe that the external world is there to satisfy our internal emotional needs, which creates unhealthy dynamics. As mentioned previously, because of subconscious beliefs from childhood, such as feelings of inadequacy, we look to external factors to satisfy these needs. For example, we have expectations that external factors such as other people or a job should make us feel happy, safe or adequate. These are illusions. Happiness, safety and feeling good enough come from within. Growing up, psychologically, is letting go of the illusion that the external world is there to take care of you or make you feel better and understanding the only you can resolve internal conflicts. It is also about accepting that you are responsible for your own happiness, contentment and the outcome of your life. If we have not resolved internal emotional needs from our childhoods, this also plays out in the relationships we have with others. For example, our childhood dynamic may have contributed to feelings of vulnerability, inadequacy and anger and instead of resolving it, we seek out ways to overcompensate and sometimes externalize these feelings. Unresolved feelings of inadequacy and anger can manifest in physical abuse, prejudices, hate crimes and the need to control others. I believe this is a huge problem in our society and many of the atrocities in the world are because we have not resolved these childhood conflicts.

There is a concept that I label as the "bully/victim" paradigm, which is an example of this dysfunctional dynamic. Based on our limited experiences, we sometimes believe that there are only two positions in the world, either the bully or victim, which are control drama paradigms learned in childhood. Some children take on the bullying position and externalize their hurt and anger on others, to release this emotion and to feel more empowered. If this child does not resolve this inner conflict, this dynamic follows them into adulthood. Some ways this is displayed is when others feel that controlling or exploiting others is a way to make them feel more powerful and in control. However, the bully is just as disempowered as the victim. The bully will then attract someone who has learned to take the victim position.

There are so many examples in which this victim/bully paradigm manifests in our lives. For example, a business owner, who hasn't resolved their childhood trauma, will likely control, manipulate and exploit their employees. An employee, who hasn't resolved their childhood trauma, will allow this dynamic and feels stuck in this situation. Or an elected official, who uses their position for personal financial gains without really caring about their constituents, will seek out and find others to manipulate. Narcissism is an example of this bullying paradigm. Individuals with narcissistic tendencies will gravitate toward positions of power. We allow this dynamic to continue to perpetuate because we are conditioned in childhood to engage in this dynamic. We then seek this out because it is on some level familiar. As a society, we continue perpetuating limiting victim-based beliefs such as "That's just the way it is," or "There is nothing I or anyone else can do about it." However, we can change this by understanding how and why we are stuck in these dysfunctional patterns, believing that there is another way and not engaging in this dynamic. As we continue evolving to this evolution in consciousness, more and more individuals will be stepping out of these control dramas which will begin changing the systems within the world.

To align with a higher consciousness, we can realize that there is a third position; not to engage in either role, and to learn how to satisfy our own emotional needs. A wise person learns how to navigate relationships without being a bully, which means not desiring power or control over others, imposing one's values on others or manipulating others to satisfy internal needs. A wise person also learns how to set boundaries with others and communicate assertively. Because most of us engage in the bully/victim paradigm, assertive communication is something that I have found to most of us don't learn. We learn either aggressive, passive or passive aggressive communication strategies. Keeping in mind that wise communication is expressed with loving kindness, let's explore the different communication styles through the following example. Your boss asks that you work overtime even though you have been putting in a lot of extra time, feel burnt out and need a break. An aggressive response would be "What the heck! Are you insane? I have been working too much as it is!" An example of a passive response would be, "Sure. I will come in," even though you really don't want to. A passive aggressive example would be, "Sure. I will come in," but then call in sick or purposely mess up at work in retaliation.

An assertive response would be "I understand that you want me to work overtime, but I am really burnt out from all the additional work. I really cannot because I need a break."

As we evolve our consciousness, we begin to understand that all interactions need to be an equal energetic exchange or a win/win situation because we are all energetically connected. When we understand that we are all connected, this impacts how we navigate the world. If we are harming or exploiting others, this affects us just as much as the other person, which is why it is so important to be mindful of our creative powers. If we are creating suffering on the planet, we are suffering as well. If one party wins and the other party loses, this impacts both parties in a negative way. A bully/victim paradigm appears to be a win/lose but is more accurately a lose/lose position. For example, corporate America oftentimes operates in this win/lose paradigm. To make profits, oftentimes, workers are exploited, the environment is destroyed, and consumers are harmed. This is not a wise business model. It is so important to understand that the negative outcomes created impact everyone. Although some may profit financially from this paradigm, there is a cost to everyone. It is unfortunate that most people do not believe that a business can be both profitable and wise, but this is not so. This is a mistaken belief system that truly needs to be changed. A wise person understands that cooperation is the only solution, and every outcome needs to be a win/win.

Exploring and letting go of addictions is another way we can start feeling empowered. An addiction is defined as a repeated dysfunctional pattern of utilizing an external factor to satisfy an emotional need. We all engage in some type of addiction. Some people escape through drugs and alcohol, thinking that a substance will alleviate feelings of sadness or anxiety. Others escape through social media, TV, technology, sex, religion, shopping, workaholism, relationships, gossip and other forms of distractions as a way of avoiding pain and emotional discomfort. Our consumeristic society is another problematic addiction, and materialism is destroying the planet. Obtaining and hoarding excessive wealth is another addition. And it is unfortunate that many admire those who are hoarding money and resources, but this is a sickness rooted in feelings of inadequacy. Individuals who obtain excessive wealth most likely are achieving this through unscrupulous means. The middle ground is always the wise choice. All these addictions keep us stuck in patterns of victimization because they reinforce the belief that the only way to cope is through external factors. Our addictions prevent us from dealing with our emotions. It is important to observe and release our addictions as a way of becoming more empowered.

Our pursuit of validation from outside sources creates suffering and keeps us from feeling empowered. It is important for us to learn that our self-worth is not defined by external sources. We frequently look to others to validate us or define who we are, or wc look for external things such as status, money, or power to define who we are. As with our expectation that external things can provide us with safety or happiness, wanting validation from external sources gives power to external factors, ones usually beyond our control. An important principle to keep in mind is that only you can validate your existence. If you are defining yourself by something external, you will be the victim of this external source. You are giving away your power.

Here is an exercise: List all the things that you believe validate your existence: your title, your degrees, your friends, your significant other, your family, your paycheck, etc. If you were to throw that list away and no longer had that degree, job, or loved one, would that change who you are? It should not. And if it feels as if it would, this puts you in a powerless place. It is important to understand that these external things can change. Are you giving up your power to external factors? This may be why you may be stuck in certain undesirable situations. For example, you may want to give up that high-paying job to pursue your life passion but are afraid because you believe the title, or the paycheck is defining your value. An inherent problem in relationships is that most of us seek validation from our partners. We sometimes want someone else to validate that we are special, possibly because we did not feel as though we received this validation from our parents. We believe that we are special only when someone loves us. However, this gives a lot of power to others. You do not need someone or something else to make you feel special because you already are. Seeking validation from within is another way in which you are powerful.

Chapter 6

Evolving into Love

As we evolve into a higher state of consciousness, we are shifting out of ego into love. Loving yourself and others is another important paradigm within an evolved state of consciousness. Because we can only love others to the extent that we love ourselves, self-love is paramount. Understanding that you are loveable and good enough exactly the way you are is the first step to self-love. Believing that we are unlovable and not good enough is a common 3-D belief that causes us emotional distress and lowers our vibration. You are loveable and good enough exactly the way you are, even if you are not perfect. Everyone is imperfect and everyone is loveable and deserves to be loved. I believe we question if we are loveable because of the messages we received throughout our lives. During our childhood, no matter how wonderful our parents are or were, most of us experienced some conditional love in our childhoods. Remember, everyone has a story. When we are born, our parents project their story onto us. For example, maybe your father was very conservative, perhaps due to his own fears, but you wanted to follow your dream of being an artist. This frightened him, and he tried to change you. In this situation, you might internalize the belief that you are not good enough, but it had nothing to do with you. Or if your parents were abusive, you likely came to the wrong conclusion that you must not be loveable if they are so angry and hurt you. Additionally, this idea of not being good enough is passed down generation to generation. It is highly likely your parents didn't feel conditionally loved and neither did their parents and so on. You may not necessarily be consciously aware of these beliefs because many of these beliefs are internalized.

One of the reasons we don't believe we are loveable or good enough is that we take things personally, which begins in childhood. As children, we truly believed the world revolved around us. We believed that everything that did or did not happen was personal. We still bring some of those ideas into our adult life. In the case of the abusive parent, when that parent is mean to a child, it has nothing to do with the child, it is the anger of the parent. The child is merely the projection of that anger. It is never personal.

As we develop, we continue to measure how loveable we are based on how others treat us. We experience rejection, abandonment, and cruelty and we continue to take it personally. However, nothing is ever personal. Nothing other people do is because of you. It is because of their internal dynamics. Remember, people do not perceive reality as it is, but as they are. No one really gets to know us because others are constantly projecting their story onto us. We are all just mirrors for other people. Rarely does anyone ever truly see anybody else because we are too involved in our own story, and we project that story onto others. How we are treated by others is because of their story and not because of us. We should never define who we are based on the action or words of others. People act in a kind or cruel manner because of who they are. People are only capable of loving others to the extent that they can love themselves. Whether someone likes you or not, it's not personal. It has nothing to do with us. Another person's behavior toward you is only a reflection of the relationship they have with themselves. Nothing is ever personal. No matter how anybody has treated you, you are loveable and good enough, exactly the way you are.

We often take things very personally in relationships, especially romantic relationships and tend to suffer when we are rejected. Unless we have done a lot of personal work, most of us will pick partners that reflect dynamics from our childhoods, which are happening on a subconscious level. Therefore, the decisions that others make have nothing to do with us, but about whether we still fit in with their story. In most cases, people rarely pick partners that are healthy for them. We usually choose partners to try to resolve some subconscious need that was not met in childhood. Because of this, what most of us think of as love is really engaging with others to satisfy our emotional needs. Now that you are embarking on the process of self-discovery and realizing that you are responsible for satisfying your own emotional needs, you may be wondering, what is love then? I believe, especially as it pertains to romantic love, that we are all on a spiritual path and each of our paths are separate. We can choose to travel together side by side, always understanding and respecting each other's paths.

Another very important paradigm shift is to start practicing unconditional self-love, which begins by taking care of ourselves. It is not selfish to love ourselves. We can only love others to the extent that we love ourselves and no one can love you unconditionally except you. When I approach the concept of self-love to my clients, most people are very uncomfortable with it, probably because we were never taught how to love ourselves. We mistakenly believe that only when we are perfect can we love ourselves because deep down inside, most of us never think we are good enough. Something I routinely explain to my clients that can assist in this process is "You don't have to always like parts of yourself or your behavior, but you always must love yourself. It is about loving the essence of who you are." For example, let's say you engage in unhealthy behaviors such as procrastinating, getting angry, or abusing substances: these behaviors are not you. They are the ways you behave. Despite the way you act, which can change, you can always love who you are.

Because we were taught conditional love, part of healing is the process of re-parenting ourselves or becoming a "good mom and dad" to ourselves. Through our psychological development, we internalize imperfect parents. We oftentimes recreate the emotional climate of our childhoods as we tend to treat ourselves like our parents treated us or sometimes the exact opposite, which isn't always better. Part of our healing journey is to make corrections to how we were parented. A good parent does not put a child in harmful situations. For example, are you working at a job that you hate or engaging with abusive people? This is not practicing self-love. We all have a hurt, scared, angry, frustrated little child inside us. Through the process of personal growth, it is important to nurture and heal that child. You can do this by being patient, gentle, understanding and observing, not judging or punishing yourself. Part of loving yourself is also about practicing self-care, such as eating well, exercising and getting enough sleep. Self-care is also about setting boundaries with others and doing what brings you joy.

Self-love is also about practicing self-acceptance, which begins with never ever criticizing ourselves for anything. As I always say to my clients, "Observe, not judge yourself," even if you are engaging in behaviors that you wish to change. Remember, these behaviors are not you. It is always important to see the inner child who is motivating your behavior. Judging or punishing yourself does not facilitate anything positive. Your job is to seek to understand your behavior. Why you are engaging in this behavior is what is important. Once you understand why, you can choose something different. Would you stop loving a child, judge them, criticize them or punish them if they were engaging in unhealthy behaviors? This would not be healthy or productive. A good parent seeks to understand why the child is engaging in these behaviors and helps them find a better solution. Again, seek to become a good parent to yourself. Every child deserves to be loved, especially you.

Self-love is also about being kinder to yourself, which starts with paying attention to the things you say to yourself. As mentioned earlier, everything is energy. Your thoughts are energy. If you have negative thoughts about yourself, this disrupts your energetic and biochemical system, which is detrimental to your health. This is why it is so important to pay attention to those things you say to yourself and practice changing them. When you begin listening to the things you say to yourself, you will likely notice how mean you are to yourself. Would you ever say those things to anyone else? Probably not. Remember your inner child and be kind to him or her.

I think one reason why many of us have a difficult time with self-love is that many people confuse self-love with narcissism. Narcissism is not the same as loving yourself. Narcissism is about only thinking of yourself and needing to feel better than others, which stems from a deep-seated belief of not being good enough. Loving yourself is not being self-centered or narcissistic, because only when you truly love yourself can you really love and care about others. When you love yourself, you don't compare yourself to anyone else. When you love yourself, you don't seek power over others or to be better than anyone else. When you truly love yourself, you also want what is best for others. I also believe that some people are afraid to love themselves as a means of self-control. Some confuse self-love with self-indulgence. But when you truly love yourself, you do not harm yourself by overindulging, like a good parent who doesn't indulge a child with cake for dinner. You practice moderation. You provide a balanced meal with a little treat. That is love. Love is never indulgent.

If you are not still comfortable with loving yourself because it feels "selfish," here is another way to look at it. Loving yourself is actually helping the world around you. As we have discovered, we are all energy and energy effects surrounding energy. Therefore, we are all connected in an energetic way. Healing our emotional scars, loving ourselves, and being happy and at peace is part of our spiritual commitment to the universe, because we are adding something positive to the universe. We are all connected. All too often, we feel that self-love, being happy or at peace is "selfish," but if we are part of a greater whole, we need to love ourselves just as much as we love others. Because we impact the world around us, being unhappy or living with fear, guilt or anger is in a sense adding negativity to our world. Therefore, it is altruistic to be happy and at peace, which we accomplish first by healing our wounds and learning how to really love ourselves. This world can definitely benefit from more love!

You may be familiar with the Maharishi effect, which has shown that our thoughts, feelings and intentions do have an impact on the world. In 1960, Maharishi Mahesh Yogi, the founder of Transcendental Meditation, predicted that if 1% of the population practiced Transcendental Meditation, this could possibly bring about world peace. Since then, there have been over 50 research studies in 108 countries that have shown that if 1% of a given community collectively practiced Transcendental Meditation, crime rate was reduced by 16% on average. This has shown that individual consciousness does in fact affect the collective consciousness.

Just like it is so important to practice self-love, it is also important to practice unconditional love for others. We can achieve this by seeking to understand others and be patient with them. Just as our unresolved emotional scars dictate our behavior, others experience the same dynamic. It is not uncommon that, once you understand your dynamic, you want others to be the same way. However, it is important to understand that others are not necessarily on the same path as you. It is impossible to change someone who is not seeking change. It is important not to have expectations and think that we can change others. All we can do is serve as an example and share with others who are interested in sharing. Remember that your expectations and the negative emotions they elicit are only hurting you. Judging others, such as thinking someone is a "bad" person, creates negative energy that only hurts you. Righteous anger is still anger and it negatively impacts you and the world around you. Keep in mind that there are no "bad" people because at our core we are all spiritual beings. Therefore, we are all connected and perfect but acting imperfectly in the human form due to our ego. People are just behaving badly, or at least in our perception, due to their emotional circumstances, such as hurt, anger and fear. We behave in certain ways based on our story. When you come from a place of understanding, not judging, this is a place of peace. One way to let go of negative emotions towards other people is to look for that inner child that is scared, hurt, angry or sad within them. It is helpful to imagine others as little children who are just replaying the human drama. Hopefully, this can shift you from anger, hurt, and frustration, to compassion, love and understanding.

Chapter 7

Evolving into Living in a Life-affirming Way

Another paradigm shift within this evolution of consciousness is to let go of fear. Fear is an illusion. It only exists in the mind. Danger is real. Fear is not. Fear is about some future incident that may or may not happen. Something to remember that you are always safe. If you are experiencing anxiety or have an anxiety or fear-provoking thought, it is helpful to remember that although anxiety feels real, it's not because nothing is really happening to you. Unless you are in danger, you are always safe in the present moment. Many of our subconscious and conscious fears keep us trapped in situations that are creating unhappiness and prevent us from experiencing love and joy. For example, if you are staying at a job that you hate because you fear that you won't get hired anywhere else, this is not real. Or if you are staying in an abusive relationship, because you fear being alone, this too is not reality. These are illusions. I think it is so important to do what you love and be in healthy situations, not what makes you feel safe. This is the difference between merely surviving and thriving.

Worrying harms the body. I believe people worry because it creates a false sense of doing something. People who worry inaccurately believe that if I am worrying about something, I am taking action. However, worrying facilitates absolutely nothing positive and impairs your problem-solving capabilities and keeps you in lower vibrational states. If you find yourself worrying, breathe, get centered and remind yourself that everything is ok, and you are safe in the present moment.

One fear that creates anxiety for many of us is the irrational belief of scarcity. Because of our experiences and the messages we receive from others, we create inaccurate beliefs that there is not enough money, love, opportunities, etc. in the 3 D world and we worry about not having enough. However, the universe is abundant and again, according to the law of attraction, we manifest that which we pay attention to. If you believe that there is not enough money, money will be an issue. If you believe that there is not enough love, love will be an issue. Therefore, instead of worrying about these concepts, which facilitates nothing positive and harms the body, start practicing changing these inaccurate beliefs.

Worrying and feeling anxious is not necessarily the same thing. It is important to discern if the anxiety you are feeling is followed by a thought or if the anxiety you are experiencing is stemming from another source. If your anxiety seems to come out of nowhere, it could be either that a subconscious construct triggered an emotional response or that this feeling of anxiety is a signal that you are not in a situation that is safe or desirable for you. If you are an empath, this can also mean that you may be feeling someone else's anxiety. It is important to get clarity on the source of anxiety, because it just may be that this is your subconscious mind trying to alert you to something that you are not paying attention to. Here are some examples to illustrate the difference. If you start to feel sick and begin ruminating about the possibility of having a horrible illness and this creates anxiety, this is an example of worrying. You can change the thought, which can change the emotional response. However, sometimes changing the thought does not change the emotional response, which indicates that it is likely triggering unprocessed emotional trauma which can be processed. However, if you interact with a person and you tend to feel anxiety about it for no apparent reason, this may be your subconscious alerting you that interacting with this person is not healthy for you or that you may be picking up their anxiety. Depending on the nature of the anxiety, this will determine your course of action. However, the emotional clearing exercises listed in the Appendix will be useful in most cases.

It is valuable to start practicing life-affirming, not fear-based living. To begin practice life-affirming living, it is important to fully embrace the idea that death is part of life. In our western world, the greatest fear that is not widely discussed is the fear of death. However, it is important to confront this fear because it's the basis of most fears. Death is usually perceived to be negative. Most people don't want to face it and go to great lengths to avoid it, which of course, is not possible. It may be that we are just too attached to the material world, which makes it difficult for us to understand that everything is temporary, even our material body. It is so important to truly embrace the reality that you and everyone else at some point will die. We usually don't know when and how, but it is the inevitable truth of being human. Because of our fear of death, many of us people spend time and energy worrying about being safe and the safety of others to ensure that nothing will happen to themselves or to the one's they love. Of course, you should take precautions such as look both ways before you cross a street or wear your seat belt while driving, but living with the constant fear of death is just not a healthy way to live. Because we are spiritual beings, there truly is no death since the essence of who you are is immortal. There is only death to the material manifestation of who we are.

Therefore, there is truly nothing to fear, and you are always safe.

According to existential psychology, to move forward in one's personal growth, it is essential to embrace the idea that we are all going to die. Death is the only thing in life that we are certain of, and we don't know exactly when it will happen, nor can we prevent it despite all our best efforts. One of the reasons that we fear death is that we fear the unknown and the idea of not being. Death is in the future and our preoccupation with it keeps us from living. However, the idea that we die can spark us to appreciate every moment we have, primarily by causing us to make choices not based on fear but based on thriving and living in a life-affirming way.

Most of us do not want to think about death, but by confronting death, we can begin to live a full, authentic, happy life. To live life fully, it is important to accept that it ends. It is sometimes in the face of death that we begin to truly live. A confrontation with death often causes us to question what is meaningful and important. Have you ever heard someone that has been diagnosed with a life- threatening illness say, "I wish I had spent more time working"? Almost everybody says, "I wish I'd spent time doing the things I wanted to do; traveling, spending time with others, being closer with my family, having fun." Many individuals experience life-altering changes after being confronted with their mortality, such as having someone close to them die or having been diagnosed with a terminal illness. These circumstances remind us that life is temporary, and we should start living it.

When you start to think about the choices you make, you will find that you make many decisions out of fear, which keeps you from living fully. Most of us live in fear and we make decisions based on fear rather than making life affirming choices. Think about the decisions that you make: are they truly positive and life-affirming, or are they created out of fear; fear of being hurt, fear of failure or success, fear of the unknown? Most of these fears are rooted in inaccurate belief systems from our past and from those around us. Living in a life-affirming way is the difference between thriving and merely surviving. Our fears keep us from living authentically. Instead of working at a job that you hate or being in an unfulfilling relationship because you believe that you need security, while wondering if you can do something you love or find more meaningful connections, choose activities and connections that bring you contentment, joy, and something that you look forward to when you wake up in the morning. Part of self-love is never staying in situations that make you unhappy. There is no such thing as security or safety in external things. These are illusions because everything in the end is temporary. What do you do out of fear? What changes can you make to live in a more life-affirming way?

Another reason we don't feel safe is that we feel the anxiety and sadness of loneliness. However, loneliness is a psychological construct because we are all connected and therefore never alone. It is not reality. It just feels real. Remember, we are energy. Our spiritual energetic self is always connected to everything. Additionally, when we come into this world, we have guides and entities from other dimensions that serve to watch over us. Therefore, we are never truly alone, we just sometimes feel alone. It is our ego self that feels separate from others and yearns for connectedness. It is important to understand this feeling of loneliness and transcend it by realizing that we are only alone in the sense that we view our experience of the world as separate. However, we are always connected to a greater whole.

You can overcome this aloneness and conquer the fear of being alone by understanding that this is only an ego construct, not reality.

In my years of working with clients, I have discovered that one of the most common experiences is the feeling of loneliness and not fitting in. I don't think that I have ever encountered one person who ever felt like they truly belonged. I feel that loneliness is a spiritual yearning for connectedness which comes from our childhood need for dependency and fear of abandonment. As children, belonging to a family was paramount to our survival. Being unloved or unwanted is a life-or-death situation. We could not survive alone in the world. However, as we grow up, we forget to move beyond this fear. We all want to be connected to a group, but we all already belong because we are all already connected. Therefore, you are never alone.

Chapter 8

Evolving into Wisdom

Another paradigm shift within this evolution of consciousness is to understand that you are wise and to learn how to trust your inner wisdom. Most of us tend to seek answers outside of ourselves, because we have been taught by the 3-D world that is where to find it. It is unlikely that anyone has ever taught you how wise you truly are and how to tap into that inner wisdom. It is also highly unlikely that anyone has ever shown you a different way of living, by looking inward for the answers. Although it is wise to seek guidance, ultimately, you need to do what's best for you and only you know what that is.

I think one of the reasons we search for wisdom outside of ourselves is because we are afraid to take responsibility and possibly make mistakes. Because of our fears, we tend to manage our lives based on what others think is best. However, we all have inner wisdom and a unique path, and no one can really show us how to live our lives. There is a Buddhist proverb that states, "Believe nothing, no matter where you read it, or who said it, no matter if I have said it, unless it agrees with your own reason and your own common sense." It is always valuable to check in with our inner wisdom and to always trust ourselves.

One of the ways to access inner wisdom is through our intuition, which is one of our most valuable assets. It's the voice of our subconscious mind also known as the higher self, which is connected to a collective unconscious. Therefore, we all have access to universal information. However, most of us do not know that it even exists. That is why it is so important to learn how to access it. One way is to learn how to sit still and access our intuition. You can learn how to ask the questions and look for what intuitively feels right, which can be learned through techniques such as meditation.

There is a powerful technique that I teach my clients, which is not only helpful in making decisions, but extremely helpful in accessing subconscious material. It is so simple, yet so profoundly effective. All you need to do is get into a relaxed state, close your eyes and take a few deep breaths. Then ask the question and wait to see how your body responds. For example, if you are wondering if a job is the right one for you, with your eyes closed, say either out loud or to yourself, "This is the right job for me." Then wait to see how you feel. Usually, the response is immediate. Sometimes you can't even say it out loud because there is so much resistance. If it is the right job for you, when you say it, there will be no resistance. It will feel right. Again, you have all the answers, you just need to sit still, uncover them and trust. Something that I have learned throughout the years is to also be patient when making a decision. We often make a choice when we don't have a clear yes. However, I believe that if it is not a clear yes, it's a no. It is wise to be patient and wait for the option that resonates with a clear yes.

You can also use this technique to test belief systems, which will be helpful in the next section where we will be working on clearing limiting beliefs. For example, if you are struggling with relationships, you may find it helpful to test your beliefs regarding relationships. Your beliefs may be the obstacle to attracting as well as holding onto relationships. When testing subconscious belief systems, the first thing I have my clients do is close their eyes and say, "I am okay being in a relationship." You will be surprised how often a client will swear that they truly want one, but when they do this exercise, there is so much resistance. Using this "okay" statement is so useful because if you are not okay with love, money, or whatever you think you are seeking, it will be difficult to obtain. These beliefs will impact your decisions and what you attract. You can then proceed further as to why relationships, money or whatever are not ok. Sometimes, we are not okay with relationships because we are afraid to lose them. Sometimes, we are not okay with money because we are afraid that we will seem greedy. I then help my clients systematically clear these belief systems by detaching energetically from them.

Intuition is where logic and emotion meet. It's the wise mind. All too often, we make decisions based on just logic. We spend hours thinking and researching but logic and information such as statistics relies on others' past truths that may not necessarily apply to you. For example, if you are thinking of getting a new job you need to find that middle ground between the logical and emotional. If you find a job that pays well and has great benefits, but you hate it, that is not the right job. If you find a job that you enjoy, but you can barely pay the bills, that one is not right either. The best job is the one that satisfies both criteria. This is also true with relationships. We tend to pick a partner for logical reasons, such as they "look good on paper;" you've checked all the right boxes but maybe you don't feel an emotional connection. Or we pick someone that we feel emotionally connected with, but they are irresponsible or emotionally unstable, and not logically a good choice. The wise choice is one that meets both the logical and emotional needs.

Part of embracing our inner wisdom is to uncover our authentic self. According to existential psychology, the existential aim in life is the individual's search for meaning and purpose through the discovery of one's authentic self. This purpose is part of our spiritual path and often we are conflicted between our soul's path and what others want us to be. Being authentic is living as who we are, not by the roles that we have designed for ourselves or that others have created for us. We are all born authentic but spend a significant amount of time wearing masks. We learn to wear these masks because we want to please those around us and to feel safe. When we go out into the world, instead of being ourselves, we desire approval, acceptance, and love from others and feel we need to wear masks to get that approval. We play a role, because we are afraid or ashamed to be our true selves. These roles are taken from images we develop of how we should be, and are dictated by others such as our parents, friends, peers or the media. Being authentic is taking off the masks that you wear and being the person who you truly are.

On some level, we all know why we are here and what we are supposed to learn and experience, but out of fear, we sometimes resist it. We try to be what others want us to be. Sometimes we are afraid to disappoint others or make others feel bad or uncomfortable. However, sometimes emotional distress, such as unhappiness and anxiety, is a signal that we are not on our authentic path. It is our higher-self or subconscious-self giving us a signal that we might not be headed in the right direction.

The key to living authentically is filtering out those other voices in your mind and finding your authentic voice. At any given moment, it seems there are several voices in your head: your authentic voice, the voice of your family, a societal voice and conflicted subconscious information. All these voices, bouncing off one another, can create inner conflict, so it is important to find your authentic voice and cast off the others. Is there something you truly would like to do, but are conflicted or fearful about? For example, are you unhappy with your current career choice, and have you always dreamt of something else, but wondered about its feasibility or practicality or believed that you may disappoint your family? It is important to determine whose voices are spreading this doubt. If your authentic self truly wants to pursue something different, it may be helpful to challenge the voices of your family and society, which may have created your fear. There will always be an inner conflict if we act to please others or do what is expected, instead of following our authentic voice. Therefore, one of the steps to an evolved consciousness is filtering out those other voices in our head and allowing the authentic self to emerge.

Once you choose to follow your authentic voice, you may feel some tension. This is perfectly normal, because frequently it is fear that has dictated your behavior. It takes courage to be authentic, and your choices truly determine the person you want to become. You have the freedom to create your own life. To be authentic also means to create your own definition of success, not what society or others deem as successful. You are responsible for your actions, but also for your failure to act. This discovery can be anxiety-provoking, because it awakens the realization that you have the responsibility to take control over your life and your destiny. But once you start practicing authenticity, this anxiety will diminish.

Part of being authentic is finding personal meaning in our lives. By living with our beliefs, we know the direction that we are meant to go, and we trust the universe will lead the way. As we learned earlier, only we can validate our existence and we must not give that power to others. This means we create our own idea of personal success and meaning in our lives. We can free ourselves from cultural expectations and create our own life, full of personal meaning. When we find meaning and purpose, all the anxiety and hopelessness and fear disappear. Our mission guides us. We become aware that we have authorship of our lives and start to take responsibility over our destiny, feelings, and even our suffering. We then create our own life meaning by creating our unique purpose in life.

Because we start to wear masks at an early age, it can be challenging to uncover who we are authentically. I have discovered two very useful tools, astrology and numerology, that can aid in helping us understand our authentic life path. Astrology is something that is very much misunderstood in our western world. Many have associated it with superstition and fortunetelling. However, astrology is one of the languages of the spiritual world as well as a psychological and counseling tool, which can be used for enhancing personal wellbeing. Carl Jung, a prominent psychiatrist and psychoanalyst, who is credited for his theories of personality extensively researched the field of astrology and even consulted the I Ching and read tarot cards.

The zodiac signs can be seen as the journey of the human experience. It represents the journey of the soul from its conception through childhood and old age. The journey begins as our soul comes into incarnation in Aries. This is where the ego and the awareness of self begins. In Taurus, our soul's journey is through experiencing the physical body. When we enter Gemini, our soul learns how to communicate with the world. In Cancer, our soul learns how to nurture others. Moving into Leo, our soul seeks recognition for its creation. Virgo represents our soul's journey of learning how to serve others and structure a daily routine. In Libra, our soul learns how to relate and compromise with others. In Scorpio, the soul begins to recognize its regenerative nature. In Sagittarius, the soul searches for meaning. Capricorn represents the soul's drive to be responsible for others through hard work. In Aquarius, the soul's quest is for humanitarian efforts. When the soul reaches Pisces, its desire is to merge with the spiritual. It is believed that we incarnate several times throughout this cycle.

According to spiritualists, it is believed that we choose the exact time and date of our birth. Our natal chart is our spiritual blueprint, which is the snapshot of the sky the moment we are born. The date of birth shows where the sun, moon and planets are located, and the time of birth indicates the position of this placement. Our natal chart gives us clues as to the life lessons we are to learn, our personality traits, our soul's purpose, and our inherent energies and temperament as well as challenges we might face. Although everyone has free will which determines their destiny, one's natal chart can indicate how someone is liable to think and react to a particular set of circumstances. One's natal chart is useful for understanding one's natural reactions and to aid in making healthier life decisions. It is important to understand that astrology is a language of symbols and should not be taken literally. Because the natal chart has so many aspects, this explains why two individuals with the same sun sign are not necessarily alike. Although our natal chart is very complicated, there are a few important indicators that can be helpful in understanding who you are authentically and why you are here. These placements include the sun, moon, rising or ascending sign and the nodes.

Our sun sign indicates our inner personality, something we don't always allow others to see, also known as the ego. Most of us know our sun sign, which represents our core personality. Aries, for example, is the first sign, whose personality is usually assertive and dynamic. Aries is a cardinal fire sign, which implies an inclination about initiating creation and change. Whereas, Pisces, the last sign, is extremely sensitive, intuitive and compassionate. Pisces is mutable water, which implies an adaptability to the environment and someone who feels emotions deeply.

The rising sign or ascending sign indicates our particular outlook on life. The rising sign is the sign that is ascending over the horizon at the time of our birth. It is our particular viewpoint based on the circumstances of our birth, the conditions of the environment we are born into and how we choose to survive during our childhood. The rising sign is as important as the sun sign because it's the mask we wear in the world and how we choose to express our core personality. With a Gemini rising, for example, one's main objective is to communicate with the world, choosing intellect and skills in communication as a means of survival. However, someone with a Virgo rising, for example, seeks to serve others, choosing hard work and structure as a means of survival.

The moon represents our unconscious drives as well as our emotional climate. It pertains to basic needs that arise from the subconscious. If one's moon is in Taurus, for example, there is an inclination to be emotionally fixed, maternal and craving security. Whereas a moon in Sagittarius, the emotional climate is more restless needing to seek freedom and adventure in the world.

Our north node is the life path or what we need to accomplish in this lifetime to fulfil one's destiny. The south node are the lessons we learned in previous incarnations that will aid in fulfilling our mission in this lifetime. Someone with a north node in Aquarius, for example, is destined to help humanity in their lifetime. Their south node would then be in Leo which represents mastering the ego and obtaining personal power in previous reincarnations. A north node in Capricorn is the path of self-discipline and hard work in this lifetime having mastered the south node's lessons in Cancer to nurture and protect others.

In addition to these four important placements, there are other planets that influence us. Venus, for example, represents our attitude with love. Someone with a Venus in Libra, for example, desires a significant other and may fall easily in love. Mars reveals how assertive we are. Having Mars in Scorpio, for example, symbolizes someone with powerful assertiveness. Where our sun, moon, rising sign and other planets sit in our chart, referred to as houses, this is how we express ourselves through both that sign and the house it is positioned in. The twelve houses correspond to the 12 zodiac signs. Aries is the first sign and the first house. The first house represents our individuality and soul's expression. The second house, Taurus, represents material wealth and possessions. The third house represents communication. It is advised that you work with an astrologer to aid in interpreting your chart keeping in mind that everyone has their own interpretation. Trust your intuition as to what information resonates with you.

On a macro level, astrology explains what we are experiencing as a collective. Astrological patterns serve to amplify certain aspects of life to make sure we are doing our spiritual and personal growth work. You are probably aware of some astrological concepts such as the full moon and mercury retrograde. Although we feel a heightened emotional state during a full moon, the full moon does not cause this. Because astrology primarily operates on a subconscious level, it merely assists in amplifying the tension that is already there in hopes of bringing it into conscious awareness.

When Mercury goes into retrograde, for example, we are aware of technological and communication glitches. This occurs because Mercury is symbolic of communication and retrogrades assist in bringing up subconscious patterns related to whatever planet is in retrograde. A retrograde storm is when several planets are in retrograde at the same time, which does not occur very frequently. However, we have experienced several in the last few years. A retrograde storm creates an energetic environment that can seem emotionally intense as we are all asked to examine things that may have been hidden in the subconscious. Collectively, we also experience shifting in nodes as well as going through eclipse seasons, which all serve to spark spiritual evolution. You may notice that during certain astrological alignment and transits, uncomfortable emotions surface. These are opportunities to continue processing traumas and clearing limiting beliefs to help us along our spiritual evolution.

Numerology is another valuable tool that can help us understand our authentic life path. As in astrology, numerology has many facets but one of the most important numbers is our life path number. To calculate your life path number, you reduce each unit of your birth date; month, day and year, into a single-digit number or a master number (11, 22 or 33). Then add the numbers together until you get a single digit or master number. For example, someone born on January 1, 2019, their life path number would be 5. It would be calculated 1 + 1 + (2+0+1+9 = 12, then 1+3 = 3). Here is a brief description of what each life path represents.

Life path 1 is the primal force. Individuals with this life path are hard workers and born leaders. They are independent and are meant to follow their own path. Individuals born with a life path 2 are the peacemakers. They seek truth, peace and harmony. Having a life path 3 is living a creative life and achieving self-expression through communication and art. They are independent, playful and have an abundance of creative energy. Those with a life path 4 are the builders and worker bees. They are grounded, serious and hard working. Life path 5 is the dynamic force. They tend to seek freedom and change and are free-skilled and adventurous. Life path 6 are the caretakers. They are incredibly nurturing and are responsible and aware of others. Those with a life path 7 are here to seek a higher awareness. They are the seekers of truth, the thinkers and are on a spiritual path. Individuals with life path 8 are here to achieve balance and power. They are excellent business executives and represent material wealth and ambition. Life path 9 is the number of global awareness and completion. They are humanitarians and take charge and care of others. Those with a life path 11 are very intuitive. They are sensitive, spiritually aware and understanding of others. Individuals with a life path 22 are the visionaries. They have great spiritual understanding and ability to apply this information in a practical way. Lastly, life path 33 are the master teachers and the spiritual leaders. They are altruistic and focused on raising the consciousness of others.

Chapter 9

Evolving into Our True Essence

As we ascend into a higher consciousness, another paradigm shift is to align with the essence of who you are, your spiritual or higher self. As mentioned previously, because you are a fractal of this interconnected energetic universe, you are connected to all. We have lost our divine connection due to programming and our life experiences, but we can begin to evolve out of ego-based living into spiritual-based living and begin living within our true essence. Spiritual-based living is the process of exploring who and what we are, and how we are alike and connected as humans. It is identifying the essence of who we are and living from our deepest nature, which includes being consciously aware of our thoughts and feelings and the impact we have on the world. Spiritual-based living is living in harmony with the universe and understanding that our spiritual essence is energy, and we are all interconnected.

Once we understand that we are all connected, we can start to perceive others, as well as our place within the universe, in a different light. It is our ego that feels separate from others and the universe, which creates distress. Distress comes in when we feel isolated and separate from the rest of the world and when we believe in an "I" against the world idea. When we shift from ego-based living to spiritual-based living, we can embrace the idea that I am part of the whole. There is safety and trust and hence no distress. There is trust that everything will work out. When we trust, we can learn that when obstacles come our way, there is a spiritual reason for it. Everything that enters your world can now be seen as a lesson to be learned, not something that you need to be upset over.

Once we shift from ego-based to spiritual-based living, we can also become more compassionate with others and understand that we are connected to one another, leading us to love each other, not hate or judge, because we understand that hatred and judgment is negative energy that hurts us just as much as it hurts others. When we hate or are angry, this just generates negativity within our universe. It is sometimes difficult to not judge and be angry when we see injustice and when others are suffering. However, peace can be attained when we understand that some, if not many, things happen for a reason, even the terrible things. We can learn to understand that others are experiencing what is necessary for their spiritual development and judging or hating those who are "bad" is still bringing negativity to our world. We can find compassion and understanding when we understand that others are possibly just following their karma. Although we may not agree with their actions, we can learn to let go of anger and judgement. Learning how to love is the goal and the purpose of our spiritual journey.

When we can put aside the ego, we come from a place of wisdom and are able to see a bigger picture. We can see that we are part of a bigger whole and can make decisions that do not merely satisfy the needs of the ego. We can put things in perspective. We can see how insignificant some of the drama that we encounter truly is in the grand scheme of things. Letting go of the ego allows us to enjoy the simple things and be grateful for what we have, not what we do not have. This concept of letting go of our ego is essentially preparing us for the ultimate letting go—death. Once we fully embrace our spiritual side, we no longer fear death, because our spirit, the essence of who we are, will always be there, even though our physical aspect may not. There is a peacefulness to be found when we understand this because much of the anxiety that we have centers on the fear of death. But if we embrace the essence of who we are, death is just the end of the material part of who we are. If we are not attached to the materiality of who we are, we can find peace in knowing that we are in a sense immortal. As we know, energy cannot be destroyed nor created, only transformed. Therefore, the essence of who you are has and always will be. Death is only the death of the physical part of who we are, not the spiritual part.

There is power in the universal flow of things and being spiritual is trusting this. It is not that we are powerless, because as mentioned before, we are the creators, but it is in our best interest to sometimes surrender and go with the flow. It is about working with the universe, not against it. If we are trying too hard, this is out of fear, which prevents us from manifesting what we want. It is not that we should not have goals, but to trust that the universe will provide a path for us, if we are patient. This idea may be foreign to us because we usually operate as though we are removed from the universe. We must do, go get things and make things happen instead of allowing the process to happen. However, you are a part of a bigger picture, and with that comes trust, because no one or nothing else has power over you. It is all harmonious. There is peace when you let go and trust that the universe will unfold its path for you. We should always strive to keep our focus on what we must do in the moment, adding something positive to the universe, and the end result will manifest itself. We tend to worry too much about the future. This worry is an indication that we do not trust that our universe will provide us with what we truly need, which is sometimes different from what we want. This wanting is attachment to the ego.

Being connected to nature is another component of living connected to spirit. Because of our modern world, we have lost this connection to nature and the natural flow of things. I really do not think we were meant to live the way we do, being so busy without time to just rest and just be. We are meant to live a life with meaning and purpose. We are meant to be creative, feel at peace and be joyful, grow our own food, commune in nature and working together in communities. Our modern life has also led us to become disconnected from each other. Working as a psychologist in downtown Chicago for over 15 years, the number one issue I would hear from pretty much every single client was a lack of community. In a city of 3 million people, most of my clients felt incredibly lonely and isolated. Even our calendar is not reflective of the natural flow of life. We celebrate the "new year," on January 1st, which is the middle of winter. Our ancestors celebrated the new year on the spring equinox because this is when the new cycle begins. Winter is about rest and healing, and we take action in spring as does the rest of nature. It is important to begin getting back in sync with the natural rhythms of the universe. Whether it is a walk in the woods or on a beach, there is so much healing to be found in nature.

Another reason that we are distressed and not at peace is because we are not living in the present moment. We are either lamenting the past, which creates sadness, or worrying about the future, which creates anxiety. Think about the moment that you are in at this minute. You are reading this book. The moment is (hopefully) peaceful. When is this peacefulness interrupted? Is it when you break away from the moment and start thinking about the list of things you should be doing instead of reading? This is judging the present. Or is it when you start wondering about what needs to be done later?

This is living in the future. Once you leave the moment, you are no longer feeling peaceful. When you start living in the future, you are no longer in the moment. When you are judging the moment, you are not living in the moment, because this judgment is created by past appraisals. Living in the future creates anxiety. Hurt, guilt, and resentment occur when we live in the past. Here is the irony. Both the past and future do not exist. They are illusions. The only thing that truly exists is the moment that you are in right now. Yesterday only exists in our thoughts; therefore, it is not real. The future certainly does not exist. If we really think about it, how healthy is it to be preoccupied by something that does not exist--the past and the future?

The moment is precious because that is all we really have. Ask yourself, are you frequently rushing through life, only focusing on the future? Are you judging the present moment in a critical way? Are you frequently upset about the past? It is vital to cherish every moment, because there is never any certainty that there will be another. You are probably thinking: Well, what do I do if the moment is terrible? Keep in mind that it is you who are labeling it terrible. It is more appropriate to acknowledge the situation for what it is, accept it without judging, and decide what you can do right now to deal with the situation at hand. Judging your reality is only keeping you from finding peace within the moment.

One of the main reasons we are not living in the moment is because we are just thinking too much. One reason we think so much is because our mind is oftentimes pursuing pleasure and avoiding pain to build a better future out of a damaged past. We think too much because we have not resolved our past and want something different for our future. It is our fear that promotes this thought process, both consciously and subconsciously. Fear is what keeps us focused on the past or worried about the future.

Living in the moment is something that we need to practice with intention, and it starts by detaching from our thoughts, which takes practice. As mentioned earlier, our thoughts become addictive. You can start practicing breaking this addiction at any moment just by deciding to be in the moment. Even if you are sitting and sipping a cup of tea, do not shift to mental autopilot, allowing your mind to race to the past or future, but rather focus on the task at hand. Be in your body, be in the experience. If you are taking a walk, focus on what is around you, feel your body and feel the experience. If you notice your thoughts drifting to something other than the present, just continue refocusing your attention on it. This is called mindfulness. As you practice, it becomes easier. When a thought or negative feeling arises, this is a sign that you are not in the moment, and all you need to do is to get centered and start again. Keep in mind, we are human beings, not human doings.

Another paradigm shift is to focus on discovering inner peace and contentment, which will ultimately lead to joy, rather than the pursuit of happiness. Most of us are taught to pursue happiness, but this keeps us trapped in suffering. Happiness is a short-lived phenomenon. We can compare it to a drug, because it has some similar characteristics. It allows us to escape the pain that we are feeling but, like a drug, the high wears off and we are left feeling the pain, looking for a way to avoid it. Many of us use the pursuit of happiness to distract ourselves from our pain. Most of us are in pain, and no amount of money, fame, or fortune can change or mask that.

You have probably said, "I would be happy if . . . I had a better job, made more money, lost weight, etc." Now imagine obtaining that which you think would bring you happiness. Sure, you would feel happy to some degree. However, when you do find happiness, it cannot be sustained; like any other emotion, we can only keep it going for a short time. Another problem with the pursuit of happiness is that we tend to search for it outside ourselves. We think that someone or something, such as a pleasurable experience, an exciting activity, or a material possession will "cure" us of our unhappiness. When we finally discover the object of our happiness, we find to our amazement and dismay that the pain does not necessarily go away. Furthermore, what happens if you don't get the job you desire or find a perfect mate? You essentially give the power to an external force that may not come through for you. Your happiness is then contingent on factors that you cannot control. Seeking happiness outside ourselves gives power over us to external factors. It is difficult to find inner peace if you do not feel in control and if you are waiting for something external to make you happy. The pursuit of happiness also generally implies that it will be found in the future. This is problematic because it diminishes the happiness that exists in the present. However, inner peace is something that you can experience right now, despite your current situation. With inner peace comes joy. Joy comes from within. It is important to pursue inner peace, which will lead you to inner joy and contentment and is something that can be achieved right now.

According to many spiritual teachings, it is believed that we are here on this planet to learn life lessons to evolve spiritually. If we are here to learn through our experiences, the situations we encounter are part of our spiritual journey. Many things that have happened in your life are designed for our spiritual growth. Understanding this can help you find peace and acceptance, especially amid adversity. As mentioned previously, many spiritual teachings subscribe to the concept of reincarnation and karma. We come back lifetime after lifetime to learn lessons to evolve in our spiritual development. We also sometimes return to help others with their path. Planet earth can be seen as a school. All of us learning different lessons at different lifetimes. Each of us in different classes, learning at different rates through our experiences. All of us are essentially learning from each other. Through relationships, adversity, suffering and our life experience, we grow. We all need to experience different aspects of human existence with the goal of learning love, compassion and understanding in the human form. We will all experience being poor, rich, man, woman, different religions, races, life circumstances. Love is the essence of our being and of our universe and the fundamental building block of nature connecting and unifying everything.

Some spiritualists believe that before we are born, we decide what lessons need to be learned in that lifetime. We pick the family and life circumstances that will best facilitate those lessons. Often our life circumstances reflect that life lesson that we need to learn. Some of us will do, what some might define as “bad” things such as murder, theft, betrayal to learn the lesson in that lifetime. Some of us will do what we would define as “good,” sometimes to rectify the “bad” things we did in past lifetimes. The idea of karma is something that we have oversimplified and is oftentimes misunderstood. Most people believe that karma implies that if you do either a good or bad deed in a lifetime, you will either be rewarded or punished in the next. As I stated before, we are not victims. There is nothing or no one out there rewarding or punishing us. We are the judge and the jury. Karma does not happen to us, we choose it. Karma is something we choose to experience in a lifetime to learn whatever we need to learn in that lifetime. Sometimes we choose a particularly challenging lifetime to accelerate our spiritual growth. Therefore, a hard life is not a punishment but rather an opportunity for more growth. This is not to mean that if you are experiencing adversity in your life, you consciously choose or deserve it. More importantly it is about understanding the lessons that need to be learned through this experience. Blaming and judging is not helpful.

Because the circumstances in our lives may be part of our spiritual journey, it is useful to keep in mind that you and your life are exactly how they are supposed to be right now and that many of the experiences you are encountering are part of this journey. Although this may be difficult to accept during a time of adversity, keep in mind that there is a reason that you and the universe have created the situation you are in right now. There is a Buddhist proverb that states "Nothing ever goes away until it teaches us what you have to learn." Through your experiences, you are learning valuable life lessons. And instead of judging them and feeling like a victim, embrace them and realize that at some time you will understand the lesson to be learned. Although it is ok to feel sad, angry, or frustrated at your situation, it is important not to stay there, but to discover what you are supposed to learn about yourself through this experience. And once you do, the circumstance usually changes.

Something I continually remind myself is, "My life is perfect, with all its imperfections. I have exactly everything I need right now. My life is exactly how it needs to be at the present." Inner peace is found when you accept your life as it is in that moment, and not in desiring it to be anything different from what it is. Even during the most trying times, you can accept the present for what and how it is without judgment and learn the lesson that is the result of the situation. You can learn to understand that the universe never gives you something you cannot handle. The situation is temporary, and it too shall pass. You can learn to trust that the universe is providing you with all that you need in the moment. Even in the most trying times, it is important to embrace the present exactly how it is and trust that what you are going through in the moment is important for personal and spiritual growth. This can help us move from victimhood to becoming empowered by the situation we are in.

It is believed that after we die our souls leave our bodies and our learning continues on higher planes of consciousness. We review the lives we have just left, learn our lessons, and plan for our next life. We choose when we will come into our physical state and when we will leave. We know when we have accomplished what we were sent down here to accomplish. After death, we have the time to rest and then return. However, part of this evolution in consciousness that we are experiencing is ending this cycle of reincarnation and clearing our karma. If we decide to come back to this planet, it will be a choice, not because of karmic lessons or debts. This is why it is more important than ever to clear our traumas from our past lives because it is our emotional attachment that keeps us locked into this karmic cycle and the 3-D matrix.

In addition to accepting our present, it is equally important to accept our past, no matter how terrible it was, and understand that those circumstances were also part of our spiritual journey. Many of us curse the past, hate the things that have happened, detest those who have wronged us, and question why these things happened to us, which leads us to feel victimized. No matter how terrible the trauma, it is important to find acceptance, because some of these situations may be part of our spiritual journey. Realistically, the past does not exist. It is only a figment of our minds. Furthermore, there is nothing we can do about our past, and being upset about it does not change things. Judging the past only creates pain for you in the present.

Many times, we hold on to the hurt, anger and resentment of our past because we want to punish those who have wronged us. But being angry only punishes us in the present and it keeps us in a lower vibrational state. We also believe that by holding on to these emotions, this will protect us in the present. But our past has nothing to do with our present or future unless we allow it. We cannot change the past; all we can change is how we feel about it in the present, and not accepting it is only negatively impacting us in the present. We can learn to embrace our past and show gratitude for those experiences, no matter how terrible. Without those experiences, we would not be who we are. It is in the face of adversity that we grow. Very little growth is achieved when things are going well for us. Without trauma, conflict, and obstacles we would have no opportunities for growth. When we understand this, we can look back on our past and be grateful for these experiences of personal growth.

Part of accepting our past is to forgive those that have hurt us. Sometimes, we find it hard to forgive others because we want to punish those who wronged us. However, holding onto this anger only punishes you. There is a Buddhist saying, "Holding on to anger is like grasping a hot coal with the intent of throwing it at someone else; you are the one who gets burned." Forgiving is really a gift that we give ourselves. Forgiveness is not a weak or passive act, but one of courage. By forgiving, you take your power back and begin living in the present moment. To feel at peace, it is important to forgive others. Often, we confuse forgiving with agreeing. However, you can still believe that if someone hurt you, what they did was wrong, and you can forgive. Letting go of the anger is not condoning what has happened. We also often confuse forgiveness with forgetting. When you forgive, you don't forget what has happened, but the negative emotions no longer follow the memory. Remember, forgiveness is not an emotion, but a choice. A choice that is important in finding peace. Sometimes we have difficulty forgiving, because we still desire that person to right the wrong, they committed. But, as mentioned earlier, those expectations cause us pain. We cannot right the wrong that has happened. Being angry, bitter and resentful keeps us stuck in a victim mentality. Furthermore, we need to remember that those experiences are possibly situations that we needed to experience for our personal and spiritual development.

However, when working through painful experiences, it is valuable not to forgive too quickly. Some say, for example, "My parents did the best they could, and I forgive them," before examining the many facets of their childhood experiences. To fully process the pain, it is important to fully acknowledge all the ways in which you were wronged before forgiving. Forgiving too quickly prevents us from fully processing all the hurt, sadness and anger. Once you have let go of the pain, the process of forgiveness becomes easier. Sometimes, we can also seek forgiveness once we understand why others did what they did. Others hurt us because they have not dealt with their own emotional demons and sometimes people just do horrible things. Again, remember that nothing is personal.

Chapter 10

Evolving the Collective Consciousness

As we evolve as a collective, it is imperative and inevitable that our systems evolve with us. Because many of our systems are built on dysfunctional ideologies and dynamics that many are no longer willing to tolerate, the world feels quite precarious. And because many have and are working through their cognitive distortions, we are currently experiencing the beginning stages of revealing the dysfunction within our systems. We are exposing the lies, corruption, manipulations and all the unsavory truths that we have not wanted to see. Because of this, our systems appear to be crumbling, and they just might be. We are creating a more evolved new world!

Many of our systems, such as our government and corporate structures, are rooted in dysfunctional dynamics that resemble our childhood, and it is because of our subconscious psychological makeup that we continue to participate in them. As a greater number of individuals evolve their consciousness, we will begin seeing significant changes in these structures, and it appears that it is already happening. For example, in the United States, we have a system of government whereby we elect representatives to make decisions for us. If you scrutinize the word government, the word govern is defined as "to rule, control or manage," which assumes that we have an inherent need for guidance, leadership and that we need to be told what to do. The foundation of this system is rooted in fear and our subconscious childlike desire of others to take care of us. Many of our systems, including our work environments, are designed on an antiquated hierarchal model, which is based on a patriarchal ideology that a select small percentage of the population is superior and has authority over others. This current ideology in government or any other hierarchal structure does not fit this more evolved paradigm. The foundation of this evolution in consciousness is to become an evolved adult, which means taking responsibility over our lives, not needing to be led, told what to do or have someone take care of us. Evolved individuals do not need or want leaders.

Within our current systems, we are essentially giving our power away and we do so because of our subconscious, and sometimes conscious, fear-based childlike desire to be taken care of and protected. Because of our victim consciousness, we mistakenly label elected representatives as "leaders," and put them into "positions of power." Our words hold power, and it is important to be mindful about how we use them. Therefore, it is wise to be mindful of how we label individuals. Heads of companies, the government, the 1%, etc. only have "power" if we assign it to them. The more we say or think about these constructs, the more we reinforce this ideology within the collective. If you examine it in terms of energy, the more attention and energy we give to these labels, the more we reinforce these old paradigms. We are sovereign beings, which implies that no one has power or authority over us. And if we want to begin changing our system, we need to change our beliefs and be mindful of our words and thoughts.

Within our current systems, unless we have self-evolved "leaders," this hierarchal model will invariably lead to dysfunctional power dynamics and narcissistic abuse. Research has shown that individuals with narcissistic and sociopathic tendencies will gravitate towards positions of leadership and the top three professions that they gravitate towards are politics, heads of companies and medicine. Therefore, a hierarchal system will inevitably result in corruption, harm and exploitation, which is exactly what we are witnessing. People who are wise do not want to lead; only those with narcissistic tendencies do. It is narcissistic to impose one's values or desire to control another human being. It is also narcissistic to believe that one has power or authority over the wellbeing of another, such as tamper with our food supply, water and air or create any rules or laws that affect another person.

Although most of us can admit that our system is seriously flawed, it is our psychological makeup that continues to perpetuate this dysfunctional model. Because none of us had perfect parents, they acted in self-serving ways to some extent or another, which created emotional distress, and our childhood wishes of being taken care of were never fulfilled. Because we project our childlike desire for "mommy and daddy," to watch over us, we tend to blindly trust figures of authority as we did our parents. Unless we have done our interpersonal work, we project these unmet needs onto figures of authority, and they become our parental substitutes. This is why we keep voting, continue working at conventional jobs at narcissistic companies, and continue participating in other hierarchal systems hoping that someone will finally do the right thing.

It is also our psychological makeup that is responsible for our cognitive dissonance which continues supporting those we have appointed as "leaders," bosses, and other figures of authority who are obviously not looking out for our best interest. Unfortunately, many minimize and even deny the wrong doings of those at the top of the hierarchy because if we were to see the reality that these individuals do not have our best interest in mind and are potentially harming us, we would then have to explore all the pain and suffering we felt as children, which is usually too much for most to psychologically handle. It is also too anxiety provoking to clearly see that we live in a world where there is so much evil and that we are all being victimized by narcissists and sociopaths. These reasons are also why we so readily rationalize bad behavior and a lack of integrity of those at the top of the hierarchy. We keep hoping that our parental substitutes will finally do the right thing.

In the 1960's, Dr. Milgram performed several social psychology experiments to understand why seemingly psychologically healthy people would blindly obey authority figures who instructed them to perform acts conflicting with their personal conscience, as witnessed during WWII. The results of dozens of experiments showed that 80% of participants would blindly obey an authority figure even if it meant harming another human being. This shows that only 20% of the population has critical thinking skills which is quite disheartening and illustrates the power of our cognitive dissonance.

Additionally, the concept of belonging to a political party is an ego-construct, as is nationalism. Because of our innate feelings of inferiority, we want to align with something bigger than us and believe we are better than others. Although we might have different qualities, skills, behaviors, etc., we are all human beings who are more similar than different. It is our ego that places judgement and seeks separation. The concept of dividing based on political ideology, nationalism, race, gender, etc. is based on a lower vibrational frequency, whereas cooperation and unity are of higher vibrational states. In some ways, part of what is transpiring politically right now is akin to a custody battle in a divorce. Some are aligning with mommy and some with daddy. Everyone is pointing their finger at everyone else, even though both parties are equally flawed. There is corruption, flaws and missteps on both sides, and neither party has seemed to solve any of our societal issues. And just like it takes a very emotionally strong and wise person to objectively scrutinize their family dynamic, the same can be applied here. A great piece of advice regarding human behavior is to never believe anything anyone tells you, look at their actions, which should be applied to political candidates. It does not matter what party is ever elected, we still have poverty, corruption, war, etc. It is narcissistic, even sociopathic, to allow our food, water and air to be contaminated. Not to mention, both parties are in support of war. War is murder plain and simple. How is this not viewed as sociopathic behavior? If we are still engaging in war, we really have not evolved as a society. The concept of having an enemy is rooted in fear-based and dysfunctional thinking and separation. You only have enemies if you believe that there are. It is an illusion.

Corporations are also mostly designed as a hierarchy and are highly narcissistic structures. It is becoming increasingly obvious that most companies are run with the ideology of profits over people. Employees and the consumers are not valued and treated as objects. Employees are dispensable and exploited and the consumer is merely a dollar sign. However, it is because of our victim consciousness cognitive dissonance and programming that we continue working at these organizations and buying their products.

Isn't the definition of insanity is doing the same thing repeatedly and expecting different results? It is becoming increasingly obvious that the hierarchal systems we are living in are just not working for the collective, and unfortunately attempting to change the system may not necessarily be a solution. Because if the system is led by narcissists, there is no reasoning or compromising with them. The only way to deal with a narcissist is to stop participating. Therefore, instead of fighting each other and the system, it is best that we just choose to stop participating and focus our attention on building cooperative solutions. For example, we have attempted to protest the government and boycott certain business, but it has not seemed to have made much of an impact.

It may be advantageous to go back to smaller communities, which appears to already be happening. Many are making the decision to opt out of conventional life and live in self-sustaining communities and this tread is likely to increase. Creating a community is also important because as a collective we all have shirked our social responsibility with hopes that the government and other entities will solve our problems. Because these systems are comprised of highly narcissistic individuals who, for the most part, only have their own interest in mind, these entities will never truly take care of society at large and it is time to release this childlike fantasy that it needs to. No one is coming to save us. It is up to us. And as we create new communities, it is important that they reflect this higher consciousness, which is based on co-operation and interdependence, not co-dependence. It is important to care for each other, not to take care of each other. Another reason that it is advantageous to go back to smaller communities is that the bigger the system, the more narcissistic the system can become because narcissists can hide in larger systems.

Regarding our work systems, we can stop buying from and working for narcissistic companies and begin creating ethical and cooperative work environments, whereby the organizations are run with integrity, and everyone is an equal contributor and valued. Within our current corporate structure, at the onset, the person who contributes the most money is the most valued. Although funding is important, without talent and labor, the company cannot grow. We should also re-evaluate our current 40-plus-hour work week and other work-related policies because they are also just not serving us. If we restructured society, we could possibly eliminate many jobs, which would reduce the number of hours people would need to work. Most jobs are not essential and are merely supporting an outdated infrastructure, as well as supporting this hyper-consumeristic society. We need farmers, builders, sanitation workers, educators, healthcare providers, etc. If we simplified our lives, this would have huge positive outcomes for the planet. Have you ever wondered why we are the only species who has to pay to live here? The indigenous cultures were so wise. They lived more simply, did not believe that we really owned anything, lived in communities, bartered and were mindful of how the planet was treated.

One of the reasons our systems have not changed is that many believe that is not possible or "realistic." However, if we understood just how powerful we truly are in that we are the co-creators of our world, we can make significant changes to our world. Although many are struggling to merely survive, which is one of the many reasons we have replayed these dysfunctional cycles for ages, however, the first step to change is very simple. It is to just believe it is possible.

Another system that is rooted in the old paradigm is our current healthcare system. The underlying philosophy of Western medicine is that we are victims of "diseases," and our bodies require external intervention for healing, which is in part why many do not take responsibility for their health. However, according to Eastern medicine, illnesses occur due to an imbalance in the body and the body has the innate ability to heal itself if given the proper environment to do so. Although natural modalities are used in Eastern medicine, no drug, procedure, vitamin, herb, or treatment heals the body. It only assists the body in doing what it does naturally, which is to heal itself. Unfortunately, we do live in a highly toxic world, which includes the food that we are consuming, which impairs the body's natural healing process as does emotional and physical stress, nutritional deficiencies, electromagnetic frequencies (EMFs), pathogens and parasites. We are, however, able to assist the body's natural healing ability by eliminating these factors.

According to Western medicine, we are also led to believe that illnesses are a result of external factors such as bacteria or viruses or due to genetic factors. The flaw in this theory is that we are bombarded by millions of germs, bacteria, and viruses daily, but become sick only when our immune system is compromised. It becomes compromised due to factors such as emotional and physical stress, nutritional imbalances, or toxic exposure. Additionally, genes may predispose us to certain ailments, but this does not mean we are victims of our genetics. Science has shown that our genes are not fixed but are mutable. Various factors, such as toxins, malnutrition and possibly even our thoughts and feelings can trigger our genes. Additionally, illnesses such as heart disease, diabetes and cancer are largely caused by lifestyle and environmental factors. In fact, 75 percent of our illnesses are lifestyle related, which puts the responsibility on us. Diseases do not happen to us but develop internally due to imbalances in our system.

We have also been led to believe that illnesses can only be "cured" through pharmaceutical or surgical interventions, which contradicts the ideology that the body is a self-healing mechanism. Pharmaceuticals are toxic to the body because they are derived from synthetic chemicals and oftentimes create many side effects. Surgical interventions are invasive and potentially dangerous and even deadly. Even psychological conditions, such as depression and anxiety, although there are biochemical and genetic factors that might be contributing to our emotional state, our gut health, thoughts, life circumstances, environment and nutritional factors play a large role which is in our hands.

Unfortunately, our mainstream medical system is a sick care system, in that it manages and medicates symptoms, does little to find causes to illnesses or empowers patients to take responsibility over their health. In juxtaposition, an alternative healthcare practitioner seeks to find the cause of the problem, not just eliminate or manage the symptoms and implements natural modalities such as herbs, nutritional supplements, dietary modifications, body work and acupuncture which supports the body to heal itself. Eastern alternatives are also noninvasive and not destructive to our bodies.

There is also a significant amount of research regarding the mind-body connection, which is not discussed in mainstream medical care. Our physical body can be seen as a reflection of our subconscious beliefs, and it mirrors to us what is out of balance. The body sometimes reflects the belief systems that we hold which are expressed in our illnesses and conditions. For example, if you are struggling with weight, this may be a subconscious need for protection. Throat and thyroid issues can occur if we are not speaking our truth. Back issues and pain can be an indication of lack of support. According to Traditional Chinese Medicine (TCM), our bodies hold onto emotional responses and store different emotions in different parts of our bodies known as meridians. For example, fear is located in the kidney meridian, anger in located in the liver meridian, low self-esteem is in the stomach meridian and resentment is in the gallbladder. It may be that unresolved feelings of inadequacy, for example, can lead to stomach disorders or unprocessed fear can impair kidney function.

One of the reasons we do not take responsibility for our health is due to our victim consciousness as illustrated previously. We have a subconscious childlike desire for our "mommy and daddy" substitutes to take care of us. Some even identify with their illnesses and are addicted to the dynamic of seeking others to take care of them. Some also would choose death over changing their lifestyle. Many are addicted to the substances they use, the food they eat and other lifestyle choices. When we grow up psychologically, we begin to understand that we are responsible for our lives, which includes the process of taking care of our health. Health practitioners are there to provide us with tools and wisdom, but we need to do the work. We have the capacity to maintain good health and overcome physical or psychological ailments. This doesn't mean that we will never get sick or die of an illness because sadly our food supply is compromised, our environment is toxic and we will be exposed to pathogens, but we do have a lot of control over other factors. Additionally, some of us, no matter how much we take care of ourselves, will in fact die of illnesses because that may be our life lesson for this lifetime. Although some of this may be inevitable, this doesn't mean we should not do the best we can to take care of ourselves.

The first step to better health is taking responsibility over our health. The second step is believing that it is possible to be healthy and in control of our health. One of the ways we take responsibility for our health is to start living a healthier lifestyle. We can do this by eating better, resting, managing stress, changing our thinking, exercising and being more mindful of the toxins we expose ourselves to, as well as educating ourselves about our bodies and health. Additionally, part of taking responsibility over your health is looking at the belief systems you have regarding your health. Do you believe that you have the ability to be healthy? Do you want to be healthy? Is there an attachment to being unhealthy, or in pain? Do you believe that getting sick is just a part of life? Do you believe that getting older means being unhealthy? Science has shown us how powerful the mind is over our health. There is numerous research proving the placebo effect. If we believe it is possible, it usually is. Part of this is not necessarily our fault because we have been programmed by the medical community, which keeps us in a victim mentality. These conscious and subconscious beliefs about our health are so important and determine our health status. You have the power to be healthy, physically and emotionally, and it begins with taking responsibility over your health.

In conclusion, although changing our systems appears to be a monumental task, we can make some significant changes by changing our belief systems about it. If even a small percentage of the collective changes their beliefs, this can have a huge impact on the whole system. Although we are programmed to believe otherwise, it is so important to remember that we are not victims of the world, but the co-creators of it. We can influence our reality by the beliefs we hold, both conscious and subconscious. If we desire to create better systems, we first need to believe it is possible. Far too many of us on this planet hold a victim mentality and believe that there is nothing we can really do to make things better. And because of our internalized victim consciousness, many have accepted the state of the world just as it is. However, you have heard the adage of whether you believe you can or you can't it is true. It is important that we truly internalize that change is possible, which begins by releasing our internal programs of victim consciousness. I understand that this isn't an easy task because these victim-based beliefs are so embedded in our DNA. We have been programmed to live in these paradigms for centuries, but we can change this. Our thoughts and feelings hold tremendous power. If we are living in fear, we are perpetuating fear. If we are feeling hopeless, victimized, we are perpetuating that as well. If we began collectively focusing our thoughts and intentions on a better world, we can manifest it. If we don't aspire to something better, how can we even achieve it.

Conclusion

Each of us is like a drop of water. Although we appear separate, we are all part of the collective. And like the drop of water that creates ripples as it flows back to its source, we have the power to affect the world around us. We are experiencing one of the most profound times in history. It is no accident that each of us is here during this epic time. We are here to not only witness this evolution but to create a blueprint for a new earth. We have the opportunity right now to manifest an idealistic and evolved world. Although we are feeling unsettled with the state of the world, it is important to continue focusing on aligning ourselves with this evolved state of consciousness and setting our intentions for the world that we wish to create. It is also important for us to remember that we are the co-creators of our reality. If we collectively focus our thoughts and intentions on a world based on love and light, we can definitely manifest it. Individually, we may not necessarily feel powerful, however, we have the opportunity to create a new earth if we all "think" together because I truly believe that there are so much more of us on the side of light and love.

Keep in mind that one of the reasons that so much chaos that is transpiring on our planet is to fully expose the shadow so that we can transmute it into light. We need not be afraid. Because light will always prevail, it is just a matter of time that we will enter a new and better paradigm, but it won't happen on its own.

There is no one coming to save us. The old system is crumbling, and we are here to rebuild it. It is up for us to stand in our power and create it. Love is the most powerful force in the universe. By focusing on love and hope, I believe we can transform the planet. We all have the opportunity right now to manifest a better world. This is truly a profound time in history on our planet. And from the ashes, the phoenix arises! Together we can spark an evolution!

It's the end of the world as we know it.
It's the end of the world as we know it.
It's the end of the world as we know it and I feel fine

- It's The End of The World as We Know It. by R.E.M.

Appendix 1

Questions to answer to help you fill in the details of your story from Chapter 4:

- What situation were you born into? What were your parents' and family member's experiences during your conception, prenatal stage and birth?
- Were there any unusual circumstances that happened around your conception, prenatal stage and/or at birth? Did you have any trauma at birth?
- Were there any significant events that occurred after you were born?
- How did your parents relate to you?
- Did you have siblings? If so, what was their experience during your prenatal stage and around your birth?

After you gather information regarding your history from conception to birth, start writing about your childhood.

- Who were your primary caregivers? What was your relationship with your primary caregivers? What was your relationship with your parents?
- What was your relationship with your siblings? What was the dynamic with them? How did you feel about them? How did they feel about you?
- How did you view yourself as a child? What was your role in the family?
- How would you describe the members in your immediate family? Extended family?
- What are some major events that transpired during your childhood?
- If you went to daycare, what was your experience? What was your relationship with your babysitters, nannies and other care givers, if you had any?

- What experiences did you have in school? During the summer?
- What were your relationships with your friends and peers?
- What were the causes of stress in your household?
- What caused you stress during your childhood?
- How did you feel about school, social activities, etc.?
- What are some memories that stand out to you?

Now start gathering information regarding your life after you grew up.

- What experiences did you have?
- What relationships did you have?
- Where did you go to school? What did you study?
- What jobs did you have?
- What are some significant life events that transpired in your adult life?
- Have you ever experienced any past life regressions? What information did you gather from them?

Appendix 2

Here are some techniques and strategies to clear emotions of trauma from cellular memory as well as energetically detaching from subconscious beliefs that are no longer serving you.

Meditation with self-energy healing

Here is an exercise to clear a subconscious emotion or a belief system by incorporating some energy work. First begin with an intention to heal a specific subconscious emotion or belief system such as feelings of sadness or not feeling good enough. Sit or lie in a comfortable position and enter into a deeply relaxed state. Take three deep breaths. Next, get in touch and feel the emotion in your body. You may experience sadness as a heaviness in your heart or the belief of not feeling good enough in your stomach, for example. Now, just pay attention to the feeling in the body. Then, imagine healing energy coming from the universe and shining a warm healing light. You can imagine white or yellow light or any other color that appears. Imagine that healing light energy absorbing the emotion or belief system. Feel the emotion or belief system start to dissolve or let go. It may create interesting sensations in your body such as tingling, warmth, or deep peace. Whatever happens, keep your focus on what is taking place. Now imagine this healing light energy taking this emotion or belief with it out into the universe far away from you and transmuting it into peace and love. Then imagine the universe infusing you with feelings of love, peace and safety. You can also ask the universe to infuse you with whatever you wish to replace such as joy instead of sadness or feeling good enough instead of not feeling good enough. You may need to do this meditation a few times to fully let go of an emotional charge.

Emotional Freedom Technique (EFT)

Here is another powerful technique that you can try that also incorporates energy points. The premise of EFT is that the cause of all negative emotions is a disruption in the body's energy system. EFT helps clear negative emotions by tapping on energy points. It works by focusing on the specific issue you wish to change while tapping on a sequence of energy points. The first thing you are going to do is identify what you would like to clear. Then rate the distress by assigning a number to it on a 0-10 scale where 10 is the worst the issue has ever been and 0 is no problem whatsoever.

Then you tap continuously on the KC (karate chop) point with your fingertips, while saying. "Even though I have this ______ (feeling of sadness or belief that I'm not good enough), I deeply and completely accept myself". Say this three times while tapping continuously on the KC point.
KC: The Karate Chop point is located at the center of the fleshy part of the outside of your hand between the top of the wrist and the base of the baby finger.

Then tap with your fingertips on the points indicated. You will tap approximately 5 times on each point. The only exception is in the beginning where the KC point is tapped continuously while you repeat the phrase you chose. The tapping is done with two or more fingertips. While you can tap with the fingertips of either hand, most people use their dominant hand. For example, right-handed people tap with the fingertips of their right hand while left-handed people tap with the fingertips of their left hand. It doesn't matter what side of the body you tap on.

Once you have completed two rounds of tapping, rate the distress again. 0-10 scale where 10 is the worst the issue has ever been and 0 is no problem whatsoever. If the distress is still there, do another round of tapping but alter the beginning phrase accordingly, such as "Even though I still feel a little sad or somewhat not good enough, I deeply and completely love and accept myself." If it increases intensity, continue doing the tapping, altering your words, until there is relief. Continue as necessary.

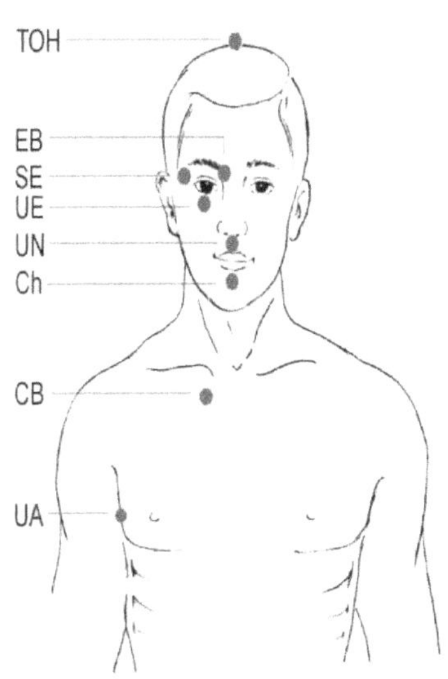

TOH: On the top of the head
EB: At the beginning of the eyebrow.
SE: On the bone bordering the outside corner of the eye.
UE: On the bone under an eye about 1 inch below your pupil.
UN: On the small area between the bottom of your nose and the top of your upper lip.
Ch: Midway between the point of your chin and the bottom of your lower lip.
CB: The junction where the sternum (breastbone), collarbone and the first rib meet. To locate it, first place your forefinger on the U- shaped notch at the top of the breastbone. From the bottom of the U, move your forefinger down 1 inch and then go to the left (or right) 1 inch.

UA: On the side of the body, at a point even with the nipple (for men) or in the middle of the bra strap (for women). It is about 4 inches below the armpit. This point is abbreviated UA for Under the Arm. 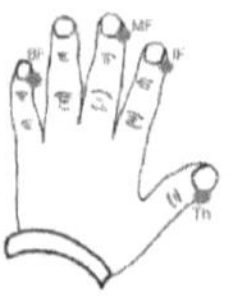
Th: Thumb point even with the base of the nail.
IF: Index finger. Tap on the side of the finger that is closest to the thumb, even with the base of the nail.
MF: Middle finger. Tap on the side of the finger closest to the index finger, even with the base of the nail.
BF: Baby Finger. Tap on the side of the finger that is closest to the ring finger, even with the base of the nail.

The Script Meditation

We all have unresolved emotions from our past and dysfunctional belief systems that are stored in our subconscious mind. Here is a "script" meditation that was edited from *Feelings Buried Alive Never Die* by Karol Kuhn Truman. This script meditation assists you in resolving these emotions and clearing subconscious beliefs and processing them by connecting to their origins. You can do this meditation as often as needed. Before you begin, think about a feeling or a belief system you would like to clear, such as feeling of sadness or a belief such as "I am not good enough". Then think of what you would like to feel or think instead such as "joyful" or "good enough". Get into a comfortable position. Close your eyes and take a deep breath through your nose and then exhale out your mouth. On the second and third breaths, inhale through your nose and then hold for the count of three and then exhale.

Next you will read the following script meditation: "I ask my higher self to go the beginning and locate the cause or reason for this feeling/thought of ___________. (Fill in what you would like to clear, e.g., unhappiness or belief that you are not good enough) Take my subconscious self to that first situation that caused this feeling to start and analyze it perfectly. Come forward in time analyzing and resolving every similar incident built upon this first situation. Fill me with light and truth, and universal peace and love and ___________. (Fill in how you would like to feel, such as happy, or think "I am good enough".) Know that every physical problem and inappropriate behavior based on the old feeling and thought quickly disappears. Take all the time you need, spirit, but quicken time and do the job now. Thank you, higher self, for coming to me and helping me attain the full measure of my creation. Thank you."

Because you may have some self-sabotaging beliefs or blocks to change or success, you may choose to first do the following meditation first a few times to clear them. "I ask my higher self to go the beginning and locate the cause or reason that I am programmed to fail... (and then continue the script until you get to the part where you insert how you would like to feel and then insert) I now allow myself to succeed. I give myself permission to succeed. I re-program myself to succeed. I am successful...." (and then finish the rest of the script). Because self-love and acceptance are very important, I would also suggest incorporating this statement a few times into your script meditation as well: "I ask my higher self to go the beginning and locate the cause or reason why I don't love myself... (and then continue the script until you get to the part where you insert how you would like to feel and then insert) I love myself unconditionally. I am worthy of being loved..." (and then finish the rest of the script). Add this statement, "I ask my higher self to go the beginning and locate the cause or reason why I don't accept and trust myself... (and then continue the script until you get to the part where you insert how you would like to feel and then insert) I accept myself unconditionally and trust myself implicitly. I am my own best friend…" (and then finish the rest of the script).

A good protocol would be to recite the script daily, clearing self-sabotaging blocks for a week, then recite the script daily incorporating self-love for a week, then recite the script daily incorporating accepting and trusting yourself for a week, and then finally work on any other emotions or beliefs you would like to clear such as feelings of sadness or not feeling good enough.

Affirmations

One of the simplest, but most effective ways to start changing your conscious and subconscious thought process is by reciting affirmations. This is a great place to start on your new self-care routine. As we have explored, you have belief systems that are stored within your conscious and subconscious mind. Therefore, the work that needs to be done is to begin reprogramming not just your conscious thinking, but more importantly, subconscious thinking. Because your subconscious mind is very susceptible to the messages it hears, if you begin saying affirmations to yourself or out loud, eventually your subconscious mind will agree with it. It might be helpful to recite affirmations everyday as a way of reprogramming your thinking.

Because self-love is so important to healing, the first affirmation that is a good place to start is "I love and accept myself." It is helpful to make a conscious effort to say this affirmation as many times as possible. It's advantageous to set aside some time in the morning and evening to practice affirmations, but they can be done at any time. Reciting affirmations may seem uncomfortable at first. When I introduce affirmation to my clients, I usually get resistance. The main response when I suggest saying “I love and accept myself,” is usually “But I don’t love and accept myself. How can I possibly say it?” However, it is important to start reciting affirmations even if you don’t necessarily believe them. In time, your subconscious will eventually hear it enough that it will eventually agree with the statement. Remember, affirmations help reprogram the subconscious mind. Therefore, I always suggest that my clients keep saying it until they start believing it. It will work. Most of us have so many fears that impact our lives. Therefore, creating a sense of safety is also important. Another basic, yet powerful affirmation is “I am safe.” Reciting this affirmation is also very helpful. Another affirmation that you can add to your daily routine is “Every day, in every way, I am getting healthier and healthier.” As you continue with your affirmations, you can create your own. Keep in mind always frame your affirmation in a positive way.

Meditation

Meditation is another very powerful tool. It is beneficial in many ways. Meditation helps us more deeply understand the different aspects of our 3 D story and detach it from it. As we have explored, we all have a script that is playing in our subconscious mind. Meditation gives us an opportunity to observe all those thoughts running in the background and to assist in detaching from them. One of the ways to achieve this is by slowing down brain processing. As mentioned earlier, our thoughts are addictive. Meditation helps in breaking this addictive pattern.

There is much research done on how meditation affects the brain in a positive way. During meditation, the frontal lobes, which are responsible for reasoning, planning, emotions and self-conscious awareness, and parietal lobes, which are responsible for processing sensory information about the surrounding world, slow down. Meditation also reduces the flow of incoming information into the thalamus, which is the gatekeeper for the senses and reduces the arousal signal of the reticular formation. When you experience a stressful situation, this triggers a reaction in the medial prefrontal cortex also referred to as the "me center." The more we meditate, the less stress we feel because we weaken the connections of this particular neural pathway. Therefore, with meditation, we do not react as strongly to stressors as we once did. Additionally, meditation helps to strengthen our lateral prefrontal cortex also known as the "assessment center," which helps us more easily rationalize our experiences. Meditation also helps the brain switch from beta wave state, which is associated with the alert mind state of the prefrontal cortex, to alpha and theta states, which induces a feeling of calm and peacefulness. It is helpful to meditate at least once or twice a day a day. Start out with 5 minutes and work your way up to 20 minutes. Find a quiet place to do your meditation practice. Get into a comfortable position. Sit with your eyes closed and make sure to keep your back straight. Start by taking in a long, slow, deep breath through your nose and then exhale out your mouth. Focus on your breathing. If a thought comes into your mind, just acknowledge it and continue to focus on your breath. You can also add a word such as peace or love or a mantra such as "I am safe," or "Breathe in and breathe out," or just focus in on your breathing as part of your meditation.

Often, when I discuss meditation with my clients, a common response is "I tried once, and I don't think I'm doing it right because I have a lot of thoughts." First, there is no wrong way to meditate because meditation is about establishing a practice. Of course, you will have thoughts while meditating. Everyone does, even experienced meditators. Meditation is not about not having thoughts, it's about not attaching to them. Meditation is about practicing detaching from your thoughts. When you are focusing on your breathing and your mind wanders, just bring your attention back to your breath. It can really be that simple. Consistency is key. Even just meditating 5 minutes every day has been shown to have positive health benefits. 5 minutes of slow deep breathing, in for 5 counts and out for 5 counts, has been shown to switch the body from a sympathetic (stressed) state to a parasympathetic (relaxed) state. Research has also shown that small segments of consistent meditation are more effective than longer periods of inconsistent meditation. You will start noticing changes once you start practicing meditation on a regular basis.

Chakra Balancing Meditation

A more advanced form of meditation is a chakra balancing meditation. There are seven chakras, or energy centers, in the body that we will focus on. Different schools of thought believe that there are more than seven. They can be described as wheels of energy located along the spine from the tip of the tailbone to the top of the head. Each chakra vibrates at a certain speed and emanates a different color. It is important that these chakras are balanced to ensure good emotional and physical health.

The first or root chakra is located at the base of the spine. It vibrates slowly, emanates a red color and controls the consciousness of survival and the feeling of being grounded and safe. During your meditation, you can focus your attention to the base of your spine with the intention of balancing it. You can picture the color red and use the affirmation of "I am safe." The second or sacral charka is located between the base of the spine and the navel. The vibration is higher and faster than the first and the color is orange. Each chakra vibrates faster than the one before it. This chakra allows us to experience joy and physical pleasure and is responsible for our creativity. After you have aligned your first charka, in your mind's eye, focus on the second chakra with the intention of balancing it. You can picture the color orange and use the affirmation of "I am calm." The third or solar plexus chakra is located in the solar plexus, right above the navel and is the color yellow. This chakra is responsible for our personal power and sense of self. After you have aligned your first and second charka, in your mind's eye, focus on the third chakra with the intention of balancing it. You can picture the color yellow and use the affirmation of "I am powerful." Moving onto the fourth or heart chakra, this chakra is the color green and is responsible for love. The heart chakra connects the physical aspect of us with the spiritual world. In your mind's eye, imagine aligning the heart chakra with the color green and using the affirmation of "I am able to give and receive love." The fifth or throat chakra is the color blue and is responsible for expressing our personal truth. You can picture the color blue in this area and use the affirmation of "I am able to speak my truth." The sixth chakra or third eye is your intuition and the color indigo, bluish purple. As you visualize on aligning this chakra with the color indigo in mind, meditate on the affirmation "I am enhancing my intuition. The seventh or crown chakra is located on the top of the head. It is the color purple, and it connects us to the spiritual world. Instead of aligning it, focus on just opening it up and meditate on the affirmation "I am connecting to my feelings of spirituality."

Sound healing

Sound healing has been used for thousands of years. The premise of sound healing is that everything has a vibration or a sound. This sound is called resonance, the frequency in which an object naturally vibrates. Each part of our bodies has its own natural resonance. Sound therapy is based on the idea that psychological and physical ailments are a result of those natural resonances falling out of tune. There are many forms of sound therapy, such as Tibetan bowls, crystal bowls, tuning forks, gongs, chanting, binaural beats, theta healing music and so many others. The vibrations from these modalities have been shown to relax brainwave patterns, focus the mind, produce parasympathetic responses such as lower heart rate and blood pressure and decrease stress hormones. Sound healing helps facilitate shifts in our brainwaves by using entrainment. Entrainment synchronizes our fluctuating brainwaves by providing a stable frequency to which the brainwave can be attuned. By using rhythm and frequency, we can entrain our brainwaves to shift from normal beta waves (waking state) to alpha (relaxed state) and even reach theta wave (meditative state). Sound healing can also help in releasing energy blockages as well as emotions that are stored in the body. If you are focusing on releasing, for example, feelings of anxiety, you can use a Tibetan bowl or work with a therapist that performs sound healing.

Yoga

Most people are aware of the physical health benefits of yoga, but yoga has so many additional benefits than just increased flexibility and overall physical fitness. Yoga is effective at improving mental and emotional health. Yoga has a similar effect on the body as meditation. The practice can help you relax, while increasing your ability to focus and concentrate, which is helpful for overthinking. In yoga, when you are moving through poses, you need to focus on your pose. If your mind wanders, you will not be able to perform the pose. Yoga is a great place to start if you want to start a meditation practice. Through yoga, you learn to slow down, breathe deeply and do one thing at a time which retrains your mind to focus on the present moment. Each movement in yoga also has a physical health benefit. Practicing a twist stimulates the digestive system. Practicing any inverted position, such as downward facing dog, stimulates the endocrine system. Yoga also has a spiritual component. Many people who practice yoga regularly feel a connection between their body, mind and spirit as well as a oneness with all. An easy way to start incorporating a simple yoga practice into your daily routine is to perform three rounds of sun salutations, which works on all the organs of the body and is a great way to get started.

Psychotherapy

Psychotherapy is effective in helping process trauma as well as identifying and changing belief systems that are contributing to emotional distress. Because you are so close to your story, it is sometimes difficult for you to see all the subconscious belief systems you hold and to find an alternate way of perceiving reality. Here is an analogy I often use to illustrate this concept. Imagine that you are wearing a set of red-colored glasses all the time, but you are not aware that you are wearing glasses at all. Everything will be colored in red. It isn't until someone points out that you are wearing red glasses that you can actually take them off and have a different perspective. Your childhood experiences and traumas color all of your current reality, which is why it is sometimes difficult to see reality any other way. Because this can be difficult, it may be helpful to seek out assistance from a therapist. The therapist can assist you by helping you take off the red lens glasses or to help you understand how your past is coloring your present reality, so that you can see reality with clarity in a safe and non-judgmental way. Let's examine how therapy works and how this is so useful in the process of self-discovery and healing.

Therapy provides a safe place for you to explore and understand all the aspects of your story, which can be scary and overwhelming especially if you have had significant trauma in your life. The therapist can provide you with unconditional positive regard in an objective nonjudgmental fashion, which we do not usually receive from the people in our lives. The therapist can also help you identify the origins of your belief systems and perceptions that are triggering emotional pain. A therapist can help you understand how you are perceiving current reality and help you relate them to your past childhood experiences to explain why you think and feel the way you do. The therapist can also provide you with alternative ways of perceiving your past and current reality to help minimize your distress. Many therapists also are trained in techniques that help process trauma stored in cellular memory such as hypnotherapy, Neuro-emotional technique (NET), Eye Movement Desensitization and Reprogramming (EMDR), Holographic Memory resolution (HMR) and others.

In addition to exploring and understanding your story and how it impacts your present life, the therapist can also help you validate your emotions. Part of the reason why your emotions are so painful is precisely because they were not validated during your developmental years. When your emotions are not validated, you do not learn how to cope with them effectively, and you tend to rationalize, avoid, or suppress them. Your emotions can also be painful because you have not learned how to soothe yourself. When your feelings are not validated, it's as if they do not matter and that can make you feel as if you do not matter. If your emotions are not validated at an early age, this can create a sense of shame regarding your emotional state, and you feel misunderstood, all of which impacts your present self-esteem. You can start validating your emotions by looking at these feelings as if you were that child, looking at them at the present time. A therapist can help with that process. Sometimes it is difficult for us to validate our own feelings, which is why it is so beneficial to seek outside help. The therapist does not judge your feelings but validates them. A therapist truly listens. External validation is a very powerful tool in the healing process. This is one of the most powerful processes that happens in therapy and why most people feel good when they talk to a therapist. Additionally, there is a cathartic effect in just sharing the story, which is so very powerful.

Another benefit of therapy is that the therapist will encourage you to feel your feelings, which is important in processing these unprocessed emotions. When negative emotions are experienced, we tend to push them away because we are either afraid to feel them or they are too painful. When you start examining your story, it is important to really feel your emotions. You may sometimes recognize this pain, at least partially, or you may push it into your subconscious because it makes you feel uncomfortable, hurt, and vulnerable. Although we all differ in the types of experiences we encountered, we all feel the resulting emotional scars that keep resurfacing. That is why it is important to work through the pain. By continually working on it and through it, you can learn how to process this pain. As you work on your exercise of exploring the past, it is important that you sit with these feelings and truly feel them, and therapy is a great place to do that. When you start to feel your feelings, feel them with the understanding that soon you will let them go. They do not have to be overwhelming, because you can control the process now that you know what you are dealing with. Feel the sadness, feel the anger, feel all the pain and, once you do, only then should you start to let those feelings go. During this process, the therapist may start using some of the mind-body modalities that I will now illustrate to help you continue to process these emotions.

Hypnotherapy

Our subconscious mind is powerful. To facilitate real change in our behavior, it is important to make changes to the subconscious mind. Hypnotherapy is a great tool to facilitate this because it works by bypassing the conscious mind, usually through relaxation or linguistic techniques, and speaking directly to the subconscious mind. Hypnotherapy uses guided relaxation, intense concentration, and focused attention to achieve a heightened state of awareness that is sometimes called a hypnotic trance. When you are experiencing hypnosis, your attention is so focused while in this state that anything going on around you is temporarily blocked out or ignored. The hypnotic state allows you to explore painful thoughts, feelings, and present-life and past-life memories that might have been hidden from your conscious mind, which helps to process emotions. Hypnosis is also useful in accessing and updating subconscious material, essentially reprograming the subconscious mind. Hypnosis can either be suggestive or interactive. It can also be a combination of the two. An additional benefit of hypnosis is that it is wonderful for general relaxation and helps relax the nervous system.

Neuro-Emotional Technique (NET)

NET is a mind-body technique that locates and removes neurological imbalances related to the physiology of unresolved emotional stress. The NET practitioner assists the client in locating unresolved emotional patterns and assists the body in processing it through either a pulse correction, which is typically used, or through a spinal correction, which is used by chiropractors. NET is based on the physiological foundations of stress-related responses. As we previously learned, the body remembers and stores traumas and compares incoming information with past experiences. According to Traditional Chinese Medicine (TCM), our bodies hold onto emotional responses and stores different emotions in different parts of our bodies known as meridians. For example, fear is located in the kidney meridian, anger is located in the liver meridian. If during your childhood you were exposed to a lot of yelling, this original trauma stored as fear, in the kidney meridian, and every time you are exposed to someone yelling, this triggers this fear, which stresses the kidney meridian. With a NET practitioner, you can go back to the original trauma and process the emotion so that it is no longer creating a physiological trigger by creating a pulse correction to the corresponding meridian which holds the emotion, in this case the kidney meridian. For more information regarding NET, please visit www.netmindbody.com.

Eye Movement Desensitization and Reprocessing (EMDR)

EMDR is a psychotherapy treatment that alleviates the distress associated with traumatic memories. The premise of EMDR is that the mind can heal from psychological trauma as much as the body can heal from physical trauma. The brain's information processing system has a natural tendency to process trauma so that it is no longer painful, but this system can be blocked by unprocessed trauma. When the trauma is processed, natural healing occurs. The EMDR clinician uses a protocol of treatment which includes eye movements or other bilateral stimulation. The client recalls the traumatic event and uses his/her eyes to track the therapist's hand as it moves back and forth across the client's field of vision or other bilateral stimulation. The client then begins to process the memory and any disturbing feelings similar to what might occur during Rapid Eye Movement (REM) sleep. The client is then asked to reframe what has occurred and the meaning of painful events is transformed. For more information, please visit www.emdr.com.

Holographic Memory Resolution (HMR)

HMR is therapeutic technique that was created by Brent Baum, an addiction counselor and clinical hypnotherapist, which is grounded in somatic and energy psychology and emphasizes the mind-body connection. The practitioner utilizes this technique to help individuals release past trauma and emotional and physical pain. Whether the trauma was a single event or repeated patterns. HMR enables individuals who have experienced trauma to access memories of these past experiences and heal from them without becoming re-traumatized or overwhelmed by painful feelings. Milton Erickson, a psychologist and hypnotherapist, suggested that emotional pain linked to past trauma could lead to a self-hypnotic state when triggered in the present. The body and mind attempt to prevent further pain by activating a state of self- hypnosis or trance states. The goal of HMR is to remove the memory storage that has taken place. By redesigning the encoding, the emotionally charged response to the memory can be altered to allow a more positive or neutral reaction. When performing HMR, a gentle hypnotic trance is induced to allow the person's conscious mind to relax and access the subconscious. Therapists frequently use guided visualization to identify the history of the presenting issue and its emotional associations, making use of color in this process. HMR practitioners assist individuals in identifying areas of the body where difficult memories are stored and helps them release these memories through emotional reframing. Individuals are encouraged to visualize events and describe the emotions experienced through colors and symbols, reimagining painful or challenging events until they no longer have the same traumatizing effect. For more information, please visit www.healing dimensions.com.

Energy healing

There are so many different methods of energy healing such as Acupuncture, Acupressure, Colorpuncture, bodywork such as Shiatsu and Thai massage, Breathwork and energy work such as Reiki and New Paradigm, many of which are rooted in TCM. As we have already learned, emotional and physical trauma disrupt the energetic flow in the body. According to TCM, energy or "qi" flows through the body along meridians. If this energy gets blocked, illness can occur, either physical or psychological. These energy healing methods release blocked qi and stimulate the body's natural healing response. Additionally, these techniques enhance communication between organs and cells. Acupuncture utilizes needles to facilitate this. Acupressure and bodywork techniques utilize touch. Colorpuncture utilizes colored lights instead of needles to work on acupuncture points. Breathwork, sometimes referred to as holotropic, shamanic or ecstatic breathwork, combines intense and accelerated breathing with evocative music to assist in releasing physical and emotional blocks by supercharging the body with oxygen and achieving an altered state of consciousness. Reiki and New Paradigm are also energy healing techniques where the practitioner is able to balance the flow of energy and releases blockages through light or even no touch. All of these methods help shift energy to process stored trauma.

Christina Samycia, PsyD is a holistic and spiritual psychologist, intuitive healing guide, author, speaker and podcaster. She has a doctorate in psychology and a master's degree in kinesiology. She experienced a life-changing awakening in 2020. Although she had been a practicing psychologist for over 15 years, she discovered that her true purpose was to be the messenger of this new age. Through her writing, speaking, one-on-one and group services, she hopes to inspire and support others to align with this higher consciousness and assist humanity in creating a new earth. She is also the author of *The Journey of Discovering Inner Peace* among other books. Christina lives in the Mt. Shasta area in Northern California with her three cats: Leo, Cleo and Star. She is available to present at conferences and offers private and group retreats and one-on-one intuitive healing services at Mt. Shasta. She can be reached by phone at (312) 285-5287 or email christinasamycia@aol.com. For more information, please visit www.christinasamyciapsyd.com.

www.ingramcontent.com/pod-product-compliance
Lightning Source LLC
LaVergne TN
LVHW010949110826
845149LV00015B/3276
9798998832208